Here for You

Creating a
MOTHER-DAUGHTER
Bond That Lasts a Lifetime

Susie Shellenberger
& Kathy Gowler

BETHANYHOUSE
MINNEAPOLIS, MINNESOTA

Published by Bethany House Publishers
11400 Hampshire Avenue South
Bloomington, Minnesota 55438

Bethany House Publishers is a division of
Baker Publishing Group, Grand Rapids, Michigan.

Printed in the United States of America

ISBN-13: 978-0-7642-0374-9
ISBN-10: 0-7642-0374-6

Library of Congress Cataloging-in-Publication Data

Shellenberger, Susie.
    Here for you : creating a mother-daughter bond that lasts a lifetime / Susie Shellenberger & Kathy Gowler.
        p. cm.
    Summary: "Encouragement and advice for building and strengthening a lifelong bond between moms and their teen daughters. Draws from biblical examples and the authors' own experience in working with teen girls"—Provided by publisher.
    ISBN-13: 978-0-7642-0374-9 (pbk.)
    ISBN-10: 0-7642-0374-6 (pbk.)
    1. Mothers and daughters—Religious aspects—Christianity. 2. Daughters—Religious life. 3. Teenage girls—Religious life. I. Gowler, Kathy. II. Title.
    BV4529.18.S535   2007
    248.8'431—dc22   2007002599

My precious mother died in 2003. I dedicate this book to
her sister, Maurine Dickerson, who loves me like a mother.
—Susie

To my mother, May Reu, I had you for only eighteen short years.
Thank you for giving me the gift of life and the gift of faith.

To Sally Gowler, my "other Mom," thank you for raising a son
to become an amazing husband.

To Matthew and Kelly, my fabulous now-adult kids. I love you
with all my heart. Thank you for the fun, the laughter, and
the joy you've brought into my life. I love being your mom!
—Kathy

CONTENTS

Susie Shellenberger is the founding editor of *Brio* magazine for teen girls, published by Focus on the Family. A former high school teacher and youth pastor, she is in demand as an international speaker and has traveled to every continent in the world.

Kathy Gowler and her husband, Jeff, have two grown children and live in Cascade, Colorado. Kathy serves as events coordinator for teen ministries at Focus on the Family and has traveled around the world with Susie.

It was over a booth of Italian food in Pueblo, Colorado, that I (Susie) had the privilege of talking with Brooke and Chrissy—both eighteen years old and in the middle of their senior year in high school. We talked about teen girls and their relationships with Mom.

Both girls are solid Christians and involved in their church. They both love their moms, but like all teen girls, they expressed frustration with communication, pressure, and a desire to grow closer to their moms as a friend.

"She used to be an authority figure in my life," Brooke said. "But now that I'm gearing up to leave for college, she's becoming more of a friend."

We'll chat about the different life stages moms and daughters grow through in the coming chapters. We'll also discuss the importance of establishing and maintaining a close, growing relationship between mom and daughter.

"My mom is my absolute best friend," Chrissy piped. "My friends love her too."

Brooke laughed. "It's true. Her mom is really fun!"

"Finish this sentence for me," I said. "I wish my mom would . . ."

Both girls thought. Chrissy chewed a bit of meatball and Brooke put her fork down.

"I wish my mom would include me with her girl friends," she said.

I nearly choked on *my* meatball. "What?!"

Brooke repeated what I thought I'd heard. "I wish my mom would include me with her girl friends."

"Brooke, that's awesome! But I have to tell you . . . I've never heard a teen girl say that!"

"Well, I've noticed that Mom has some really genuine friends. They're women I admire. Every now and then they go out to lunch or they'll get together and paint. It's really cool."

I smiled . . . imagining her mom would light up if she knew this. "Brooke, have you shared this with your mom?"

"No."

"Why not?"

"She doesn't know that I'd like to be a part of that, and it would be hard for me just to . . . you know . . . bring it up. It would feel weird to ask to be included."

I couldn't help but think of my friends who have teen daughters and how they'd feel as though they'd won the lottery if they had any idea that their daughters would enjoy spending time with them and their friends.

And I remembered a conversation I'd had with seventeen-year-old Mallory a few years earlier. "You and my mom have been friends since college," Mallory said. "I want to go to a Christian college just so I can make some genuine, lifetime friends with Christian girls. I want what you and my mom have."

Moms, does this surprise you?

Daughters, will you take the initiative, if necessary, to tell your mom what you need and want from her?

As you hike through the pages of this book together, both of you will be asked to take the ultimate challenge of a lifetime. You'll be asked to make a covenant: moms, with your daughters; daughters, with your moms; both wrapped in a holy relationship with God.

When this sacred mother-daughter covenant is truly understood and lived out, it changes everything! The crisis in homes due

to the lack of understanding, failure to trust, and unnecessary sep-
aration between moms and daughters will fade.

This covenant will affect *everyone* in the family, and you'll read
stories of how it has changed lives.

Chapter 1

"I'm Not Ready for This!"

I remember my mother's prayers and they have always followed me.
They have clung to me all my life.
—Abraham Lincoln

Let's have a heart-to-heart here. You're reading this book because you want to strengthen the bond between you and your teen daughter.

Living with and attempting to raise well-adjusted responsible teens is a frightening task. There are certain issues that automatically come with the territory of being the parent of teenagers, particularly for the mom of a teen girl. Recognize this and you'll be prepared in advance to deal with these issues.

> "I love it when my mom spontaneously gives me a hug and tells me she loves me."
>
> —Courtney, 17

No question about it, you have your hands full. Whether you're happily married, have a difficult marriage, or are a single mom, balancing life as a mother is exhausting. Many of you hold down a job, plus you're carpooling kids to ball games and keeping hungry mouths fed, clothes clean, dogs washed, bills paid . . . Maintaining a household and raising a family is work!

With little or no time to yourself, it's easy to become frazzled, frustrated, and *fatigued*! What kind of superwoman does it take to do it all?

Know Your Limits

In the hectic pace of life in the twenty-first century, there are still only twenty-four hours in every day—the same amount of time in every day that our grandmothers had and their grandmothers had before them. What our generation expects to accomplish in that amount of time has become unrealistic and unreasonable.

Computers, microwaves, dishwashers, and fast food are supposed to make our lives easier and free up our time, but the reality is, we only work longer and harder to get more done in any given day than ever before. The result is families short on time together and long on reasons to be frustrated with each other.

> "I love when my mom makes an effort to join or be interested in my activities."
>
> —Hillary, 15

There may come a time when you have to make some tough decisions to cut some things out that really aren't as important as your family thought they were.

We can only do so much. God never intended our families to be frazzled and stretched so thin that we don't enjoy being a family at all. The family sitting together around the dinner table at night is becoming a rarity that may happen one or two nights a week at best.

And if you have in that home an adolescent daughter with raging hormones, mood swings, an insatiable appetite for her cell phone, and no time to clean her room, a tired mom with not enough hours in her day is a time bomb waiting to explode. Dad and brothers, run for cover!

Sound familiar?

Calgon, Take Me Away!

One thing is certain—there *will* be stress in your life! Some of it you can prevent, some you can't. We'll let you in on a little secret here: It is possible to learn to work *smarter*, not harder. That will mean different things to each one of you, but the key is to look for ways to lighten your emotional and physical load so you can enjoy these crazy teenage years to their fullest. Not only will *you* reap the benefits, but so will your entire family. A calm and refreshed mom can be the biggest stress-reliever for the entire household.

If you want permission, you'll get it right here: **It's okay to say no.** There are other people out there who can head up the bake sale for the band or teach that Sunday school class at church. You are the only mom your family has—they need you and deserve your attention more than anybody else.

So here's your assignment. Ready? You may want to take notes so you don't forget.

"I love it when my mom plays with my hair, goes to lunch with me, or watches a girly movie with me."

—Sabrina, 20

Make Time for Yourself

At least once a week, indulge yourself with an hour just for you. Go someplace quiet and read a book; take a long, hot bubble bath (hang a "do not disturb unless the house is on fire" sign on the bathroom door if you have to); go to lunch with a friend or to the mall by yourself—and don't feel guilty about it.

Have your nails done.

Whatever it is that refreshes you, make the time to do it. You will be a better mom because of it, plus you're modeling to your daughter that it's healthy and necessary to take time for yourself so you can be at your best for those you love. To better love others, you need to first love yourself.

DO THIS. It's important! *You're* important, and you're doing an important job in raising your family.

Then Came "Tweens"

It's very likely you woke up one day to find some monster entered your house during the night and stole your sweet young daughter and replaced her with a total stranger who argues, slams doors, rolls her eyes, and cries over everything.

Congratulations, you're the proud mother of a tween girl!

Possibly the toughest, definitely the most awkward phase of growing up is the "tween-age" years—the years between ten and thirteen. No longer a little kid, not yet a teenager, your tweenager struggles to find her place in this world.

"I love it when my mom smiles and tells me I did a good job."
—Mandi, 17

We live in an age where the childhood years have shrunk. Some of our precious little girls are going through puberty as young as nine and ten years old. Their bodies are changing from child into woman earlier than ever before. One day she's playing with her Barbies, and the next she's horrified to see breast buds forming and hair starting to grow in places she's not ready to think about. Her body is telling her she's becoming a woman, but her age and her world are those of a little girl.

This can be a very confusing and frightening time, especially if she's not prepared for what is happening to her. As her mom, make it a point to be in tune with what's going on in your tween daughter's mind and body. You can't depend on the school nurse to teach your little girl about things of womanhood. You need to be ready to approach this topic sooner, not later.

When you start to see her body changing, be the one to walk her through it.

She'll have questions.

Give her straight answers.

Don't beat around the bush and awkwardly stumble through the same lame "birds and bees" explanation your mom may have given you. Kids are smart today. If you don't present the issues of puberty to her in an understandable way, she'll either ask her friends (who may not tell her the way you want her to hear it) or do her own research on the Internet.

> "I hate it that things go unresolved between us. There have been times Mom has really hurt my feelings and I told her, but it sure was hard. Not much changed, so I probably won't tell her again."
>
> —Latisha, 18

Be Prepared

It's our privilege and responsibility as moms to introduce our daughters to the facts of life and the changes her body will experience as she develops from an awkward, gangly child into a lovely young woman.

Don't let this important moment sneak up on you.

Be proactive and ready.

Know your daughter well enough to know when it's the appropriate time and how much she's ready to hear. Chances are she already knows more than you think she does and is dying to know the truth from someone she can trust—her mom.

Powerful People

Statistics show that tweens, more than any other age group, have the attention of the marketplace. Some will even say that tweens have the most spending power among all age groups. They are not yet able to drive or get a job to fill their empty hours, so parents give them money to go to the mall, movies, or amusement park to keep them entertained.

Peer pressure to have what their friends have drives insecure and inexperienced parents to dish out the dough to keep their powerful adolescent content. Tweens are masters of argument and quickly learn to use the guilt card on the mom or dad who appears to be "out of it" and old-fashioned.

"*Everybody* has an iPod."

"*Everybody* has hundred-dollar designer jeans and two-hundred-dollar athletic shoes."

Really?

Cosmetic and entertainment companies market products to this age group knowing full well the spending power they have, much to the frustration of their parents.

Ever notice how many cosmetic products on the shelves today are geared to entice the ten- to twelve-year-old girl? They scream, "You're not cool if you don't use this at your age!" from their trendy and enticing ad campaigns. Many moms fall for the line that all the other girls at school are wearing it. Your young daughter is not the only one in her class who still looks her age.

There is such beauty in innocence. Don't rush into making your little girl grow up too fast.

Your tween has a greater engagement with the world through

"I love it when my mom laughs. Her nose crinkles up really cute."

—Tori, 15

media and technology than we ever did at her age. She's being lured and marketed to from every angle. Some back-to-school products geared to the adolescent buyer come with lip gloss and eye shadow.

Be prepared and know how you're going to deal with this kind of pressure before you find your eleven-year-old leaving for school looking like she just had a cosmetology lesson from the lady on the corner downtown, and we're not talking about the Avon lady.

"I love it when my mom lets me use her as a journal."

—Janie, 17

Make it a point to be the one to introduce your daughter to skin care and the world of makeup and cosmetics. Here are some practical ideas to help get you started:

Make a Day of It!

Take her to a department store cosmetics counter where she can learn how to care for her skin and how to apply makeup that is age-appropriate. You may tell her in advance that this will be a special event on her thirteenth birthday or whenever you determine is the right time for your daughter to enter this part of the grown-up world. This can be a fun "rite of passage" event that the two of you can celebrate together.

Be intentional.

Be purposeful.

Be the one to walk your daughter through the doors of childhood into womanhood.

Tweens want to be older than they are and will push your buttons, driving you to exasperation trying to get there if you let them. Decide in advance what the rule of your home will be when it comes to issues like entertainment and movie choices, clothing, makeup, and boy-girl parties.

Education has changed.

The days of being told to obey your parents are gone.

Our kids are taught at a very young age to question everything. They'll argue with you and question you, your family rules (you better have some!), and your motives. It *will* happen. Don't let it catch you off-guard.

Learning to Be Independent Doesn't Happen Overnight

A smart mom will realize that letting go of your daughter is a process that happens over a period of years. You don't turn her loose the minute she turns thirteen, expecting her to make rational adult decisions.

Teach her how to handle the new responsibilities that come with being old enough to go out without you— things like obeying curfews and family rules, calling home when she gets to the mall with her friends, and being where she's supposed to be when it's time to pick her up.

Kids don't simply become responsible by accident. They need to be taught, guided, and corrected when they make mistakes. As they prove they can handle one responsibility, you give them more.

"I love it when my mom teaches me how to cook."

—Erin, 17

Being independent is a responsibility that is learned and earned by experience. As your young daughter learns how to handle responsibility and independence, be careful not to give her too much at once. And be sure to praise her when she handles it well!

Be Ready for Conflict

Don't kid yourself. If you have teenagers or soon-to-be teenagers, there *will* be conflict. They want to grow up; you want "the good ol' days" when it was just you and them eating PB and J sandwiches and watching *Sesame Street*.

They want more freedom and independence; you're watching theevening news about all the dangers lurking out there in a big scary world.

You set up boundaries, and they think you're being unfair and over-protective.

Plan ahead.

Don't let conflict scare you; it's a natural part of any relationship where there is more than one opinion involved. Establish this early in your home: You're the parent, not your daughter's best friend.

When she's older (in college or married), the friendship part of your relationship will come. During her teen years she needs you to be her mother, not her friend.

"I was really mad at my mom because she wouldn't let me go out with friends she didn't know. But later, she helped me see it through her eyes, and I saw that she was right."

—Abigail, 15

Be Forgiving

Your daughter *is* going to blow it now and then. She's learning what it means to handle herself away from your watchful eye, and she'll make mistakes in judgment from time to time. She didn't learn to walk without falling a few times, and she won't learn to be a responsible young adult without messing up now and then.

Don't hold it over her head when she does. Many issues of conflict between teen girls and their moms stem from Mom's inability to give her the benefit of the doubt and believe in her to do better next time when she messes up.

Give her another chance to prove she's learned from her mistakes. It will save you both boatloads of conflict and stress.

Listen!

You know and I (Kathy) know that moms have the innate ability to do ten things at once. We can put in a load of laundry, frost a cake, and make a mental grocery list all while keeping the eyes in the back of our head on our toddler and hearing all about our daughter's most terrible day ever at school.

"I love it when my mom tells me that I'm her precious, beautiful daughter no matter how I look."

—Kara, 19

While you may hear every word about that most terrible day at school ever, if you don't *appear* to be listening, your daughter will likely roll her eyes, stomp off to her room in a tearful huff, and accuse you of not caring about her life that's falling apart.

A teen girl's life can have a tragedy every other minute depending on the time of the month or the way her hair decided to go that morning.

Try to give her your full and complete attention when she talks to you about what's going on in her life. If you're not listening to her with your eyes, she thinks you're not listening to her at all. Look at her when she talks to you.

Give her your full-on attention for those few moments when she's sharing her heart with you.

If you don't, she'll go to her friends or the boy down the street. At least *they* actually listen to her.

Be Generous With Your Praise

"I love it when my mom has tea with me and we talk about theology and politics."

—Ericka, 20

You know how it feels to have done your best at something, put a lot of extra effort into it, and no one seems to notice? You're not too motivated to do it again, are you?

If you go to work day after day, month after month, doing your best to meet all of your boss's expectations, even going the extra mile and putting in long hours, never hearing a word of praise, you soon get discouraged and burned out. What's the point? Nobody seems to care.

Your daughter lives in a pressure-cooker world just like you do. She may not have a boss, but she has parents and teachers and coaches who expect a lot out of her often without a word of praise or acknowledgment of a job well done.

She's *expected* to do her part, just like you're *expected* to do your job.

Know what?

A little praise can go a long way. It's true for us as working adults, and it's true for your teen daughter. She needs to know you notice how hard she tries and when she succeeds.

It's easy to notice when our kids didn't make their bed or pick up their mess. They sure hear from us when they don't do the dishes or vacuum the house when we ask them to, don't they?

Try praising your daughter just for doing what she was *expected* to do. When was the last time you praised her simply for being a good kid or for remembering to turn the oven on when you asked her so dinner would be ready when you got home? We all need to be appreciated and affirmed, *often*.

It's a dog-eat-dog world out there in the workplace, in the classroom, and on the school bus. Take time to notice what your daughter does right and let her know you're proud of her. It'll go a long way to solidify the close relationship you want to have with her.

Let Her Discover Who She Is

Do you have a tomboy daughter who'd rather play tackle football with the guys and wears nothing but jeans and sweatshirts while you envisioned shopping for cute skirts and matching shoes? Many moms stir up so much unnecessary conflict with their daughters over this very thing.

She's athletic; you want her to be girly.

She's outdoorsy and loves caring for animals; you want her to play the piano or learn to sew.

She's uncooperative and you're frustrated.

Let's ask a simple question here: Whose life is it, anyway? Know what, Mom? You've had your teen years. Now you need to let your daughter have hers. You may not even realize you're trying to relive your own teen years through your daughter. Just because you were a cheerleader and head of the pep squad doesn't mean she wants to be too.

Take a minute and evaluate why you want your daughter to be a specific way or involved in certain activities. Are they *her* passion or yours?

The Gift She Longs For

One of the greatest gifts you can give your daughter is the freedom to discover her unique passions and abilities. If she loves to tinker with motors and can fix the family car, let her! You may love your hymns, but she's into contemporary Christian music. Be thankful she's not into profane rap! Choose your battles carefully.

If it's not a moral issue, agree to disagree on some of these matters of personal taste. Be careful that you're not trying to make her into a clone of you. God has created her to be beautifully unique. Give her permission to explore who she is without your trying to make her be something she's not.

Think About It

- Am I parenting with purpose, or simply trusting everything will somehow take care of itself?
- In what specific ways am I encouraging my daughter to be who God created her to be?
- After reading this chapter, I feel . . . (a) overwhelmed, (b) I'm on the right track, (c) I need to make some adjustments, or (d) I'm glad God is in this with me!

CHAPTER 2

"Issues? Of Course!
I'm a Mom and I Have a Teen Daughter!"

*Any astronomer can predict with absolute accuracy just where
every star in the universe will be at 11:30 tonight. He can make
no such prediction about his teenage daughter.*
—James T. Adams

It's funny really.

Just because we walk around in adult bodies, it's assumed that we've put away childish things. But the truth is, we're all little girls inside. Many of us still carry vivid memories of those fragile childhood days when we were just discovering life and something or someone deeply hurt us. And the hurt we're talking about is the kind that scars you for life.

There's not a Band-Aid or ice-cream cone in the world that can make it better. You remember it as if it were yesterday.

"I love it when my mom knows something's wrong without my having to say anything."
—Tawni, 14

You know just where you were when it happened.

You remember the smell of what was around you.

You carry it into your adult life no matter how hard you try to put it behind you.

You're horrified that you've become your own worst memory. The way you parent your children is reminiscent of the painful past you try so hard to forget. Maybe you can identify with one of these young girls.

Never Measured Up

"I love it when my mom reminds me before school every day that I'm the King's daughter."

—Allie, 17

Was this you? Your cousin Elisabeth seems to get all the attention from the adults because she has dimples and beautiful blond curls. Your hair is dull and lifeless, and try as you might, you just can't pull a dimple out of those pudgy little cheeks of yours.

Your own mother says *Elisabeth* will turn a lot of heads someday.

Deep inside you know she's wishing she could say the same about you.

Even her name is beautiful. *Elisabeth.* It rolls off your tongue with sweetness and elegance.

Right away you learn that you'll never measure up to her. Your whole life will be spent in her shadow.

You feel helpless and hopeless, destined to a life of being ordinary and unnoticed while *Elisabeth* is sure to succeed in whatever she does. The unfair lottery of genetics just didn't make you a winner. Your self-esteem is shattered, and you're only six years old.

The "D" Word

Maybe you're more like Marianne. Her home was dysfunctional. While other kids' parents took them to the park or skating with their friends—even to McDonald's on Saturday mornings—her mom worked two jobs, leaving Marianne to watch her little brothers while Dad lay passed out on the couch from his drinking binge the night before.

If he talked to her at all, it was to yell at her for not keeping the boys quiet or to command her to bring him another beer. Mom was always exhausted and had all she could handle just to keep food on the table and gas in their old broken-down car. She had little energy left to notice the sadness and longing in her daughter's eyes to have a normal life and go to the park like the other families. Neglect and Rejection became her two best friends. She'll never deserve anything more.

"I love it when my mom turns up the radio and sings at the top of her lungs."

—Ellen, 14

A Masquerade

Jody had it all. Her parents had a big house, new cars, and a swimming pool. Dressed in the latest styles, she caught the eye of all the jocks with her flowing long hair and figure that curved in all the right places. She had the perfect life, or so it seemed.

Nobody knew that Jody actually loathed her life. Her parents were never home—always rushing off to some party or meeting at work, leaving her to occupy her time in front of the TV or on the phone with her friends.

Out of sheer boredom and hunger to be loved, she said yes to every guy who asked her out, and there were plenty. The attention was what she craved. Soon she felt the sting of rejection when jock after jock took pieces of her innocence and then left her for the next girl to come their way.

Before long, she was used and abused over and over again. To survive, she got very good at playing the game of pretend. She pretended she was happy.

Pretended it didn't matter how many guys used her and dumped her.

Pretended she *liked* having the reputation of being the school's party girl. The truth is she was bitter and angry.

Deep inside she began to hate men. They had their fun, then tossed her away like a dirty pair of socks. She quickly learned she couldn't trust her heart. She couldn't trust men. Real love was an illusion. The fairy-tale kind of forever love she saw in the movies was just that, a fairy tale.

Bitterness ruled her heart.

She'll probably marry someday; that's what you're supposed to do. But she'll never totally give her heart away again. It's too painful. She builds a wall of protection around herself.

No one will ever break her heart again.

"I hate it that my mom and I argue every single day."
—Seminole, 15

Past Guilt

Patty did the unthinkable. Pregnant at fifteen, she found a way to make this bad dream go away. Her parents would never even know. In a dingy office two counties away, her problem was erased.

No more baby.

No more problem.

Now her boyfriend would still want her.

No one told her she'd be haunted with guilt the rest of her life. Her boyfriend—the one who said he loved her and wanted to prove it—didn't hang around. No one told her that every time she saw a mother and baby it would make her want to vomit. Her stomach would wretch like it all just happened yesterday.

She was scum.

She was a murderer.

God would never forgive her; she would never forgive herself. She would have to keep this horrible secret for the rest of her life. No one would ever know.

Unattainable Perfection

Cindy grew up in the parsonage. Her father pastored a large church, and her family was greatly respected around the community. They were God-fearing people who didn't sin.

They read the Bible and were examples of what Christianity was all about.

They followed the rules.

They walked with their heads high.

She was a good girl who obeyed her parents and never did anything wrong. She would marry a God-fearing man and raise God-fearing children. Her home would be one of order and discipline.

"Children are to be seen, not heard. They're properly punished for their infractions. That's God's way."

That's what her mother always said.

"I love it when my mom takes me on errands with her without anyone else just so we can talk."

—Stacia, 16

Get Rid of Your Baggage

Although we may look like we have it all together on the outside, many of us carry around heavy baggage of low self-esteem, rejection, bitterness, self-loathing, and unrealistic expectations of perfection. It not only drains the life out of us, it can suck the life out of every relationship we have, especially the relationship with our young daughters.

Jump ahead fifteen years. Each of these broken little girls are now grown up with children of their own. They've become mothers of daughters who are blossoming into young women faster than any of them could have imagined.

Unfortunately, their own past experience makes them believe it will be no different for their daughters than it was for them. The task of parenting a teenager is frightening.

Life is unfair.

Better get their girls ready for it.

Your cousin Elisabeth *did* turn heads. She had all the boyfriends while you sat at home with your parents on Saturday nights. She was a cheerleader and got a college scholarship.

Your mom said it would happen.

She was the gifted one.

You were "sweet."

She married the hunk, lives in a big house in the suburbs, and has an exciting career.

"I love it when my mom puts her arm around me without saying anything."

—Hannah, 15

You eventually married Roger, who works hard to provide you with an ordinary house on South Any Street in Smalltownville, USA.

You should be happy for that. After all, you get what you get. You're content to sit on the back row of life and watch while the smarter and prettier ones are on stage.

You'll never sing in the choir or volunteer to head a committee. You want to stay unnoticed, thank you. No one will be disappointed with you there.

One day you wake up to the fact that you have a teen daughter who looks more like you than Elisabeth. The family genes didn't come through for her either. To protect her, you encourage her to play it "safe." She mustn't put herself out there to be rejected.

It's better to hang around the fringes where she won't be noticed.

It won't be as painful that way.

But somehow she makes it on the debate team in school. It probably won't last, and you tell her so. After all, it's better to prepare her for failure than to give her false hope. She needs to learn to be content with who she is.

It's only a matter of time, and she'll be married to a hardworking man like your Roger and live across the street from you in Smalltownville, USA.

That's all we can expect out of life. We're not *Elisabeths*.

What's at Risk

The Mariannes and Jodys of this world who are now mothering daughters may not do it intentionally, but the message they send is loud and clear: "Don't trust men, they'll only disappoint you. I've been hurt, and you will be too."

"It frustrates me when I try to cook a meal and it never seems good enough for my mom."

—Stephanie, 16

The rejection and pain of their own pasts are carried over to influence what their daughters think about men.

Whether it's rejection from your father, a bitter divorce, or past mistakes, you must not assume your daughter's life will take on the same heartache that yours has had.

Don't set her up for failed relationships and distrust of men simply because that's what happened to you. You can trust God with her life and ask Him to protect her from the heartache that you've known.

Her life can be a brand-new start.

Guilt Cripples

If you're a "Patty" and carry the burden of guilt from past sin, the temptation is to hide behind a mask of secrecy and shame. Guilt can be crippling.

Your heavenly Father wants you to know this: No matter what you've done, He wants to free you from your guilt. You don't need to carry it around another minute.

All you need to do is hand it over to Him and ask His forgiveness for your sin.

Maybe you've already asked God to forgive you, but you can't seem to forgive yourself. You live with the memory of your mistakes, and it's almost too much to bear.

Every day you slip on your mask to hide the pain. It's a matter of survival.

"I love it when my mom remembers the special days in my life."

—Rondi, 15

You're trapped and tangled in the web of the Accuser. Satan is the enemy of your soul.

He won't let you forget.

He doesn't want you to be free.

He'd love nothing more than for you to pass on to your children the legacy of secrecy.

If they ever knew the truth about you, they'd be repulsed. You're repulsed with yourself.

You're convinced the only way you can survive is by hiding the truth of what you've done.

You worry about what people would think if they knew.

Do you know that you're not the only one who's been there? What if you could drum up the courage to ask a godly woman to pray with you about releasing your burden of guilt? Start by asking God to bring that woman into your life—someone you respect and can trust to keep your confidences.

God never intended us to walk this Christian journey alone.

Legalistic Perfectionists

"Cindy" moms can do so much damage to their children by setting the standard of unrealistic expectations of perfection and what they perceive Christianity is supposed to look like. She's the one whose daughter won't talk to her about what's really going on in her life.

It would freak Cindy out to know that her daughter has been throwing up after she eats because she feels fat.

She'll also be the mom who proudly announces to her church friends that *her* daughter got first place on the quiz team and in no uncertain terms proclaims that she and her husband would *never* let her go out with a boy alone until she's sure he's the one she's going to marry.

She has no idea her daughter resents having to be on the quiz team (she'd rather play basketball) and sneaks out with her boyfriend behind her parents' back every chance she gets.

Cindy thinks she's being a good mother and is protecting her daughter from the evils of the world. She believes she needs to control her children, and she believes they won't be tempted to try worldly things if they're not exposed to them.

"I love it when my mom sneezes. It's so cute."

—Cassie, 18

That's the way she was raised, and that's the way it should be.

Sadly, her unbending and overprotective methods of parenting only seem to push her daughter further away.

Communication between them is reduced to arguments over

too many rules and lots of slammed doors. Instead of raising a "good Christian girl," she finds herself with a rebellious, angry young woman on her hands.

There's Hope for Change

With the birth of your daughter comes a brand-new opportunity—a clean slate. She's a completely blank canvas! You have the privilege and responsibility to make sure the baggage you carry from your own childhood isn't passed on to her.

You have the power—through covenant—to break the mold of your own insecurity and past failure and equip her to become a strong, confident young lady who will not only pursue her dreams but has a chance at achieving them.

Before that can happen, you must have the courage to face your own issues and determine not to let them drag you down any longer.

You may say, "How is that possible? It cripples me!"

Here's the secret: You have a Creator who's crazy about you!

He smiled when He formed you in your mother's womb.

He took delight in the shape of your nose and the way your smile is just a bit crooked on one side.

"I love it when my mom sits with me in church."

—Robyn, 14

He rejoiced in the roundness of your frame and the twinkle in your eyes that you think are set a little too far apart.

He created you in His image: a woman of inestimable value and worth. His heart broke when someone made you feel you didn't measure up to a prettier, slimmer girl.

He has dreams for you.

Dreams you never had for yourself.

He wants you to know that it's never too late to shed the pain of the past and start over with confidence and true *contentment* in who He created you to be inside and out.

Yes, God sees your pain and knows where you've been. He gave His Son's life for you to make you whole. Only His love can heal your past and give you wholeness and deliverance. This may not be easy.

Do you have the courage to be transparent with God and face your past?

You can receive His free gift of healing and watch Him throw your shame into the sea of forgetfulness.

He wants to wrap His arms around you and bring you to a place of complete healing.

You don't have to hide behind your pain anymore.

Bottom Line

"It's really tough when my mom thinks I'm being disrespectful. What I really want is for her to just listen to me. Sometimes she doesn't really hear me unless I go into crisis mode."

—Alexia, 18

It's really true: We live what we learn.

The way our parents reared us will greatly influence the way we parent our own children.

Some of us intentionally decide we're going to rise above our own circumstances and do things differently with our children. Others don't give it much thought, and before we know it, we've become our own mother, saying and doing the very same things that we hated so much when we were teens.

The thing to remember is this: How you choose to raise your children and interact with them is up to you.

Which will it be: "Good enough is good enough. At least it's not as bad as I had it" or "I'm going to chart a new path for my children, teaching them and preparing them for life with intentionality so they don't carry the same baggage I did"?

Did you notice that last one? "The same baggage I *did*." The key is to move on from your past and not to make your kids suffer from your mistakes.

What's done is done.

We can let our children learn from our mistakes.

They already know their parents aren't as perfect as we pretend to be.

By letting them see how we've risen above our failures through God's power, we're equipping them to do the same when they blow it.

Your childhood and teen years are over. Your daughter's life is a brand-new adventure.

It's *her* adventure.

You can choose to help make her teen years a joyful journey (which takes work and a lot of prayer), or let things happen as they may, inviting years of struggle and conflict for the whole family.

It's a choice.

> *"I love it when my mom helps me clean my room."*
>
> —Lori, 16

You'll either parent with purpose or parent by default. Much heartache will be avoided if you make the decision to be a smart, purposeful parent, leaving your pain behind.

Think About It

- Do you feel good about how you're parenting in relation to your own childhood experience?

- Identify one positive change you can make now about your parenting techniques.
- Do you identify with any of the moms in this chapter?
- Is there anything from your past that's crippling you?
- Are you willing to let God have your pain so you can move beyond it to be an emotionally healthy parent?

Father God,

I recognize that there may be some things in my past that are influencing the way I parent my own children. Please give me the courage to face them honestly and move toward wholeness and healing with your help.

Amen.

Stuff I Wish My Mom Would Tell Me

- *how to find the right bra size*
- *how to make my hair look better*
- *that she loves me no matter what*
- *that my opinions are important*
- *how to use a tampon*
- *why I'm growing so fast*
- *how much money we have or don't have*
- *that she'll always be there for me*
- *that's she's proud of me*
- *that she thinks I'm talented*
- *how to get people to like me*
- *how to know for sure if a guy likes me*
- *sexual things; I know the facts of life, but I still have lots of questions.*

CHAPTER 3

"Of Course She Has Issues, She's a Teen Girl!"

You teach your daughters the diameters of the planets and wonder when you are done that they do not delight in your company.
—Samuel Johnson

It's a Different World

It's a volatile combination, a sure recipe for drama, tears, and potential disaster.

Take one normal, well-adjusted young female.

Add three parts unpredictably changing hormones.

Mix with three parts peer pressure.

Fold in three parts parental expectations, four parts insecurity, and a dash of low self-esteem.

Toss into an ever-changing and confused culture, and what do you have?

A teen girl.

Our daughters live in a much different world than we did at their age. We worried about things such as who would ask us to the prom and the big project due in class next week.

Teen girls today worry about terrorist attacks, the weird guy who watches them walk to school, and the friend who is cutting herself and abusing alcohol.

It may shock you to know what's really on your daughter's mind every day as she walks out the door to school. Her life is bombarded with pressure to be noticed, sexy, and popular.

That's what it takes to be successful.

She's heard it all her life.

Pick up any teen magazine or flip on MTV. The message is loud and clear. Average isn't good enough. You have to turn heads. You have to achieve.

Our generation is producing teenagers who are a hybrid of waning traditional family values mixed with liberal tolerance and postmodernistic thinking. They're taught to question everything and find their own belief system, even creating their own religion if they want—whatever works for them.

While many things are different in the life of teens today, some things will forever be the same. The teenage years have always been and will always be full of change, change, and more change.

Changing bodies.

Changing hormones and emotions.

Changing styles.

Changing social and cultural standards.

Changing laws and gas prices.

Changing expectations from parents and teachers.

Dealing with so much change can be frightening and overwhelming. Although they'll never ask for it, teens need loving support and the security of their parents' life experience to help navigate the turbulence.

"I love it when my mom makes my favorite casserole."

—Haley, 18

Are You in the Know?

How well have you kept up with what's current in the world of teenagers today? Check out these facts about the culture your teen daughter is living in:

Top Social Concerns:
1. Education
2. Child abuse
3. Drunk driving
4. Racism
5. Drug abuse

Top TV Networks:

Guys:
1. Comedy Central
2. ESPN
3. MTV
4. Fox
5. The Cartoon Network

Girls:
1. MTV
2. The Disney Channel
3. The CW
4. Nickelodeon/Nick at Nite
5. ABC Family

Top TV Shows:

Guys:
1. *Family Guy*
2. *The Simpsons*
3. *SportsCenter*
4. *Chappelle's Show*
5. (Tie) *South Park, CSI, That '70s Show*

Girls:
1. (Tie) *The OC, That's So Raven, Gilmore Girls, CSI*
2. *One Tree Hill*
3. (Tie) *The Simpsons, Full House, 7th Heaven*

Top Radio Formats:
1. Hip-Hop/Rap
2. Current Hits
3. R&B
4. Country
5. Hard Rock/Heavy Metal

Top "In" Activities:

Guys:
1. Going to the movies
2. Going to college
3. Having a girlfriend
4. Playing sports
5. Dating

Girls:
1. Going to the movies
2. Going to college
3. Shopping
4. Going to the beach
5. Dating

Top Magazines:

Guys:
1. *Sports Illustrated*
2. *ESPN* magazine
3. *Game Informer*
4. *GamePro*
5. (Tie) *Sports Illustrated for Kids*, *Official Xbox Magazine*

Girls:
1. *Seventeen*
2. *Teen People*
3. *CosmoGirl*
4. (Tie) *People, Cosmopolitan*
5. *Glamour*

Top Online Activities:

(*besides IMing and emailing*)
1. Playing games
2. Researching for school
3. Surfing for fun
4. Sampling music clips
5. Looking for stuff to buy

Top Web sites:
1. Yahoo
2. Google
3. MySpace
4. Hotmail
5. (Tie) Xanga, eBay

Top Music Acts:
1. Usher
2. Ludacris
3. (Tie) The Game, Green Day
4. T.I.
5. Eminem

"It was really hard to hear that my mom had been molested. I'm glad she told me, though. I know it took a lot of courage for her to talk about it. Now I feel as though I can tell her anything."

—Kellye, 18

Top Catalogs:

Guys:
1. (Tie) Eastbay, CCS
2. JCPenney
3. L.L. Bean
4. Eddie Bauer
5. Victoria's Secret

Girls:
1. Victoria's Secret
2. JCPenney
3. Eastbay
4. Delia's
5. (Tie) CCS, L.L. Bean

Top Income Sources:
1. Parental handouts
2. Gifts
3. Odd jobs
4. Part-time jobs
5. Allowances

Top Chain Clothing Stores:
1. Old Navy
2. Hot Topic
3. American Eagle
4. (Tie) Aeropostale, PacSun

Top Durable Items:
1. Yearbook
2. (Tie) Cell phone, MP3 player
3. (Tie) Digital camera, sunglasses
4. (Tie) Used car, backpack
5. Contact lenses

Top Cell Phone Uses: *(besides talking)*
1. Checking time
2. Text messaging
3. Calculating
4. Playing games
5. Taking photos

Top Coolest Brands:

1. Nike
2. Sony
3. Abercrombie & Fitch
4. (Tie) American Eagle, Hollister

Top Candy Brands:

1. (Tie) Reese's Peanut Butter Cups, Starburst
2. Skittles
3. (Tie) Snickers, Hershey's Kisses[1]

How'd you do? If there were few surprises, congratulations for being in touch with today's youth culture! If you didn't have a clue, you might want to watch and listen more closely to what the teenagers in your home are doing and saying.

"I love it when my mom tells me she loves me."

—Kelsey, 18

What Are They Really Dealing With?

Christy's a size fourteen. She wants to be a size two. Size two girls are cheerleaders. They look great in anything—tight jeans, midriff tops, short skirts. The boys notice size twos. Size fourteens might as well be invisible.

She'll do whatever it takes. Maybe then she'll be noticed. Maybe then she'll feel worthy.

Yes, if she could just be a size two, heads would turn.

Boys would call.

Her dad wouldn't look at her in disgust.

Her brother wouldn't call her "Amazon Girl."

Whatever it takes.

---

[1]Information taken from Teenage Research Unlimited, 707 Skokie Blvd., 7th floor, Northbrook, IL 60062, *www.teenresearch.com.*

She'll drink water and chew gum. Who needs lunch?

She'll work out two hours a day and get home too late for dinner.

Whatever it takes.

Whatever it takes. . . .

Size two.

If she could only be a size two, her life would be perfect.

––––––––

Emily fears being made fun of by the teacher who mocks anyone who dares to disagree with his liberal beliefs and defends a faith of their own.

He laughed at her for saying she believed in the Creation. Most of the class laughed too. No one came to her defense as he verbally ripped her to pieces.

She'll never stick her neck out like that again no matter what her youth pastor says.

God must be disappointed in her.

She's disappointed in herself.

––––––

"I love it when my mom gives me a genuine compliment."

—Natasha, 16

Amber fears her mom and dad's continual fighting will end in divorce. They don't even trust each other.

She wonders if marriage is worth the trouble. Who needs it? Might as well just live with someone and have an easy escape when things get tough.

Less complicated.

Less hassle.

If they divorce she'll be asked to take sides. Who will she choose?

Her dad's threatening to move across the country.

She doesn't want to lose her friends or change schools. Mom is depressed and no fun to be around.

She wishes she could just run away from it all.

———————

For Sarah the pressures are overwhelming.

How will she pay for college?

Will she even get into college?

She's expected to achieve and do well on the SAT; she knows how much her parents need her to get that scholarship. Their dreams for her are huge, and they tell all their friends what a good lawyer she'll be someday.

She doesn't want to be a lawyer.

She's not even sure she wants to go to college.

They don't even ask what she wants to do with her life. It's all been planned since the day she was born.

They don't even know who she is.

———————

Mandy's coach expects her to be a star. He says she has the natural talent and physique, and he offers to spend his evenings training her.

But something about the way he looks at her makes Mandy uncomfortable.

He offers to drive her home.

Mom and Dad think it's great that

"I felt like my mom was talking for me everywhere we went and treating me like a baby. Eventually, after many tears and talks, I understood that she was an external processer and was proud of me, and I was taking it the wrong way and thinking she was telling everyone my life story when I didn't want her to."

—Annabeth, 14

he takes such a personal interest in her. If they only knew. . . .

———————

Senior Skip Day is coming up and the class is having a camp-out on the beach. Cindy knows there will be alcohol, drugs, and guys and girls sleeping together. If her parents knew, they'd never let her go.

Her friends are pressuring her. After all, she's eighteen and an adult! She can do whatever she wants, right?

If she doesn't go, she'll be the laughingstock among her friends and lose any chance she has to be prom queen.

If she goes, it means lying to Mom and Dad and losing their trust.

She's confident she can handle herself and not give in to alco-hol and sexual advances like her friends will. Mom and Dad never need to know what really goes on at the beach that night.

Her gut is wrenched in torment.

She loses either way, or so she thinks.

———————

Megan has a horrible secret. On the outside, her life appears to be perfect—she's a good student, has lots of friends, and was even voted "most likely to succeed." Her parents are proud.

They don't know what happened at the party that night.

They don't know about the rape.

They'll never know about the abortion.

She disgusts herself.

The only way she can live with the pain is to inflict more pain, so she presses a knife against her wrist and opens her skin.

Watching herself bleed brings a strange kind of relief.

She deserves it.

She took an innocent life.

There are no words to describe the horror of what she's done.

If anyone ever found out, they'd hate her for sure, just as much as she hates herself.

More Than They Can Handle

Self-destructive behaviors such as eating disorders, drug and alcohol abuse, and self-mutilation are rampant with teens today. It may be hard to understand, but teens who hurt themselves intentionally do it because it makes them feel better emotionally. They're overwhelmed with emotions such as sadness, depression, anger, or the feeling that they have no control over their lives.

Self-destructive teens have often been abused—physically, verbally, emotionally, or sexually. Not knowing what to do with these strong emotions, vulnerable young people sometimes resort to inflicting physical pain on themselves for temporary relief. Focusing on physical pain gives relief from the emotional pain.

Ask your teen daughter how many people she knows who are involved in these types of harmful behaviors. She'll know some, and you may be shocked at her response. It's even possible she's been sworn to secrecy by a friend involved in a harmful lifestyle or relationship.

"I love it when my mom wakes me up in the morning by massaging my back and saying softly over and over, 'I love you.'"

—Lauren, 14

Suicide is the leading cause of death among teens and youth ages ten to nineteen years old. Hopelessness and depression are devastating emotions that need to be taken seriously.

Most of our kids know someone personally or have heard of

someone in their school who has given up on life and done the unthinkable.

Add to this mix graphic movies filled with cursing, porn, and illicit sex; vulgar lyrics in popular music; confusion about gender roles, same-sex marriages, and bisexuality. It's no wonder our kids are stressed out and searching for honest answers and a reason to live.

A wise parent will acknowledge the vast differences between the culture you grew up in and the one your teen daughter is thrown into every day. Make it a priority to know what's going on in her world and how it affects her emotionally.

Determine to be a safe place she can run to when the world is full of confusion and life seems out of control. She needs you to understand the world in which she lives. Get out of your comfort zone and be there.

"I love it when my mom sings to me and treats me like her best friend and not a kid."

—Emily, 16

Tune In

Most likely your daughter's not going to offer detailed information about what's going on in her life that troubles her. She may not even realize that she *should* be troubled by some of her peers' behaviors.

She spends the majority of her day being influenced by those outside your immediate family—by teachers, friends, and media. It's easy to get mixed messages about what's normal, acceptable behavior and what is not.

So what can you do to protect her from harmful things that are influencing her?

Establish Clear Boundaries

Hopefully by the time your daughter's a teenager, the family rules and behavioral expectations are well defined. She knows what you approve of and what you don't.

Most kids really do want to please their parents. It's when Mom and Dad seem impossible to please that teens simply give up. It's so important that your daughter knows how proud you are of her for being compliant to the family rules.

Believe it or not, in a culture of broken homes and parents too busy to care, it's actually somewhat of a status symbol for teens to check in with their parents if they're going to be late. It proves that their parents *care*.

If you don't require her to be accountable for her whereabouts or curfews, she's in control, not you. She may act like she doesn't like it, but knowing that you are concerned about her safety will give her security and confidence.

Open Communication

You may have had the sad experience of growing up in a home where communication was one-way: Your parent spoke and you listened. Remember how that angered you? Your opinion was never sought after; your ideas were never heard.

Open communication with our daughters is critical for an honest and healthy relationship. That means we don't do all the talking; we *listen*. In fact, you may need to listen far more than you talk.

Give your daughter the freedom to say what she feels without fear of being criticized or argued with. If she feels safe talking to you, even when what she says may shock you, she'll be more likely to open up.

The truth is, we hear from teen girls everywhere we go that they wish they *could* talk to their moms. Many feel like they simply can't without Mom trying to solve all their problems or get involved.

Sometimes, your girl just wants to talk. Let her.

You'll gain a wealth of knowledge about what's going on with her friends, at school, in the youth group, at the sleepover, or wherever she's involved just by listening to her talk.

No advice needs to be given.

Just listen.

Nothing Off Limits

Wouldn't it be great if every teen girl could talk to someone about the deepest things in her heart, and that person could be her *mom*?

Imagine if she knew there was one person who would always shoot straight with her and give her an honest answer to the many questions going through her head—questions about life, her body, sex, marriage, childbirth, you name it.

If she knew she could go to her mom with questions about *anything*, why wouldn't she?

Sadly, many teen girls feel they can't talk to their moms about certain things. It's "too embarrassing" or "my mom would never talk about such things."

Know what? Your daughter may not be asking you, but she's asking somebody.

At *Brio* magazine, we get hundreds of questions by email every week from girls asking us—total strangers!—things they should be asking their moms. Things like,

"I love it when my mom prays for me."
—Suzanne, 14

"How do you use a tampon?"

"What's a training bra?"

We've even had questions such as:

"Is it true that if you French kiss a boy you're no longer a virgin?"

Seriously!

Why aren't these girls asking their mothers these questions? If they can't even ask about a training bra without being embarrassed, they'll never ask their moms about their menstrual periods or a yeast infection—things every girl needs to know about as she's growing into womanhood.

Commit to being the one person your daughter can ask questions of, knowing she'll get an honest answer.

Be Sensitive, Not Nosy

Suppose your daughter comes home from school one day, slamming the door behind her, walks right past you through the kitchen to grab a snack, and abruptly retreats to her room, slamming yet another door. Your mother-instinct wants to run in after her and find out right then and there what's going on.

Did she flunk a test?

Did she not make the volleyball team?

Did her best friend die in a car accident?

It's pretty obvious she's upset and doesn't want to talk about it. At least not right now.

Your barging into her room and asking a million questions about her day and begging her to tell you what's going on is not likely going to result in her asking you to sit on the bed and talk it through with her.

If she wants to be alone, let her be alone. Chances are, when she's ready, she'll talk about it.

When she's ready.

Be there without being nosy.

Give her some space. She'll come to

"It was tough when a close friend of mine died. It didn't seem as though my mom felt very compassionate. We talked it out, and I now realize that we process grief differently."

—Lanelle, 19

you when she needs you. If she knows that you are her safe place when the world gets a little too crazy, she'll come.

Sometimes she won't need to come.

She'll figure it out for herself.

And that's okay. That's *very* okay.

Think About It

- Moms: Are you really in touch with the world your daughter lives in, or are you living in the past? If you're still in the past, are you willing to get out of your comfort zone and step into a world unfamiliar to you so you can be a safe haven for your daughter?
- Daughters: Do you take advantage of your mom's life experience and ask her for support when you deal with tough cultural issues? Are you willing to take a risk and talk about the tough stuff with your mom?
- Moms: Are you too nosy? Do you give your daughter space when she needs it to work things out for herself, yet she knows you're there for her if she needs you? Work on finding a healthy balance.

CHAPTER 4

The Power of a Covenant

A mother understands what a child does not say.
—Jewish Proverb

The next couple of chapters define covenant making. Why is this important? Because a sacred covenant has the power to change everything between a mom and daughter. So we're asking you to wrap your arms around the next two chapters and embrace the biblical truth. It's important.

Really.

Why? Because a covenant is much more than a decision or a promise or a commitment or a pledge or an agreement.

It's even more than a contract. A contract always has an ending date. A covenant never expires. A contract usually involves one part of a person—a specific skill, a certain job to be done, an agreed-upon amount of money. But a covenant involves the totality of a person—his or her total being.

The word for *covenant* in the Old Testament comes from a Hebrew word that means "to cut." After making an agreement with each other, two people would often walk through the slain body of a heifer. They would walk right over the blood, symbolizing, *I'm relinquishing my unique identity to this person and intermingling his identity with mine. I'm giving up my rights to simply being me. I now have another person who is part of me, part of my identity.*

(Don't panic, there won't be a challenge to do a bloody walk together as mother and daughter.)

Often they would cut themselves on the wrist and grab forearms to mix their blood with one another. We'll get more into the specifics of different kinds of covenants in the next chapter. But right now, let's take a glimpse at how a covenant between two friends changed a man's self-esteem forever.

"I love it when my mom hugs me and tells me she loves me. I witness her love for me every day, but feeling that reassurance always brings great peace."

—Natasha, 16

Yes, covenants are that powerful. Because spiritual covenants are holy—and are made through God—they have the power not only to boost self-esteem but also to change lives, alter destiny, and provide immense security.

That's how it happened with someone in the Old Testament.

And that's how it can happen with you!

The Guy With the Odd Name

His name was Mephibosheth.
Unknown. Obscure. Rejected.
But the men he was connected to were extremely well known.
Successful. Admired.

The story actually begins before Mephibosheth was even on the scene. It begins with the main characters of David, Jonathan, and Saul. You may be familiar with the story.

Saul was the king of Israel. God had specifically placed him in this honored position of leadership. He started out right. He was well respected by his peers and successful in battle. When he accepted the throne, he was serving God. But when Saul took things into his own hands, the King of Kings quit blessing the earthly king and placed His hand instead on a young shepherd boy named David.

Yes, David tended sheep.

But he was also a musician.

A warrior.

And a young man who loved God.

In fact, he loved God so much, it broke his heart when he learned that Goliath—an abnormally large Philistine soldier—mocked and cursed God. David, still in his teen years, couldn't stand the fact that no one was fighting for God's honor.

He approached King Saul and volunteered for the job. Saul's armor was too big and bulky for this teenager, so David merely used what he had: his faith in God and the slingshot he'd used through the years protecting his flock of sheep from wild animals.

Yes, he was good with a slingshot.

Yes, he'd had a lot of practice.

But it wasn't simply skill that made him a winner that day as he faced the giant.

Nor was it luck.

Or fate.

Or coincidence.

You see, God had spent David's lifetime thus far preparing him for just this moment! While David was wrapped up in the ordinary task of caring for smelly animals, standing in the hot sun, moving sheep from one patch of grass to

"I love it when my mom rubs my back."
—Becca

another, God was working through the ordinary to create the extraordinary.

The same is true with you!

Don't be discouraged with the mundane details of your ordinary life. While you may not see purpose or the bigger picture, God is busily working inside the events of your life, preparing you for something extraordinary.

But the key?

It's how you handle the ordinary days that determines your extraordinary ones.

Instead of despising the day-to-day, learn to rejoice in it. Grow to love the ordinary schedules and responsibilities you have and strive to respond to them in extraordinary ways. When God sees that He can trust you with the ordinary, He'll know He can trust you with anything!

"When I first became a teen, I thought I was all that, but Mom kept me level-headed, showed me that I wasn't in charge, and loved me through discipline."

—Amber, 17

A David Type of Love

Ordinary teen.
Only one among many brothers.
No one special.
But he loved God, and his heart broke when God's name was cursed.

Chances are you love God too. May we take a moment to examine that love before we move on?

Do you love Him with a Sunday-morning love? A once-a-week Bible-study love? A part-of-a-big-church love?

When His name is cursed on television,
in movies,
in print,
or by your co-workers,
does it break your heart?

Or . . . have you become used to the mockery?

God wants you to love Him with a David-type love. He wants your heart to break when you hear His holy name, His character, or His identity being mocked.

Will you pray that God will help you fall more and more in love with Him every single day of your life? Once you're truly in love with the Creator of the universe, something very interesting begins to happen: The giants in your life no longer seem abnormally large. In fact, you become blinded to their size; it's no longer an issue how tall, strong, wealthy, or powerful they are. Those are things you no longer notice.

What you *do* see is God's mighty power working in and through your life to accomplish immeasurably more than you can even imagine (see Ephesians 3:20).

David gathered five smooth stones . . . as he had every day of his life that he'd been tending sheep. Again, he was simply involved in the ordinary details of his life, but he was about to witness the extraordinary power of God *through* the ordinary.

There he stood—Goliath—probably close to ten feet tall. But David wasn't focused on size, strength, or power. He was focused on simple obedience. He placed a rock in his slingshot and pulled it with all his teenage might. And you

"I love it when my mom shares her special chocolate with me. And I absolutely adore it when she asks me for fashion advice."

—Rachel, 14

know the story—the rock hit Goliath right in the temple of his forehead, and he never even saw stars. He died immediately.

David rushed to the giant's side and cut off his head. And like any ordinary teen guy would do, David carried it around town like a trophy for show-and-tell.

Word Gets Around

Of course, King Saul was ecstatic! He admired David's skill and even had him enter his court as a special musician to play privately for him.

Saul's son, Jonathan, also admired David's accomplishment, and the two became fast friends. Really, more than friends—they became as brothers. Even more than brothers—they became soul mates.

And as the years passed, God revealed to David that he would be the next king. He would succeed Saul. David became more successful in battle and popularity, and Saul became jealous. Intimidated even.

And as Saul walked away from God's will, he began to plot David's death. Jonathan heard about the plan and warned David. Before David fled for his life, though, he and Jonathan made a covenant. A sacred oath.

They agreed to care for one another's family as if they were their own. Through the holy blood covenant, they took on each other's identity. In obedience to God, Jonathan relinquished his human right to the throne and assured David of his total support as the future king.

The men embraced, and David fled.

"I love it when my mom makes my favorite meal for me and sends me mail in college."

—Anna, 20

Fast-Forward

I hope you'll take time to read this fascinating account in its entirety, because we're leaving out several parts of the story to move along and highlight how powerful the covenant was and is. (You can find the entire story in 1 Samuel 17–31 and 2 Samuel 1–9.)

Fast-forward several years. Saul and Jonathan were both dead. David had been on the throne for a few years, and he was enjoying a successful reign. He was wealthy. He was happy. He was fulfilled.

Probably one evening standing on his balcony after a favorite meal, he may have been overlooking his vast land and counting his blessings while his thoughts flashed back to his friend Jonathan.

Imagine David lifting the sleeve of his royal garment and running his fingers across the scar on his wrist. *The covenant. The eternal covenant I made with Jonathan. I told him I would care for his family as though they were my own! I wonder if Jonathan has any family still living.*

Disturbed by this thought, genuinely wanting to keep his word, and being eternally bound by his holy covenant, David began to seek information about Jonathan's family.

He learned that Jonathan had a son who was still alive. His name? Mephibosheth.

We're taking this story right out of the New International Version of the Bible. It may appear differently in the version you've chosen to study right now, but in the NIV, Mephibosheth is first mentioned in 2 Samuel 4:4. And no, he's not mentioned with capital letters—Grandson of King Saul or Son of Well-Known Jonathan. He's mentioned in parentheses! Look it up. Mephibosheth is introduced to us in *parentheses*!

Let's take a look:

> *(Jonathan son of Saul had a son who was lame in both feet. He was five years old when the news about Saul and Jonathan came from Jezreel. His nurse picked him up and fled, but as she hurried to leave, he fell and became crippled. His name was Mephibosheth.)* 2 Samuel 4:4

How would you like to be described in parentheses . . . and defined by your weakness?

(Cynthia, the one with the bad marriage.)

(Karen, she used to have a drinking problem.)

(Janet, she's been divorced twice.)
(Abbie, she struggles with an eating disorder.)
(Lindsey, the one with the learning disability.)
(Krista, she's the one who's easy with guys.)

Mephibosheth is mentioned again in 2 Samuel 9. And when he's mentioned again, his life will change forever. That's where the power of the covenant comes in. But before we get to that point, let's think about how the King of Kings views *you*.

An Everlasting Love

No doubt you're aware that God loves you. You've heard it. Read it. Maybe even sung about it. But have you accepted it? *Really* accepted it?

Are you living your life by this great truth?

The King of Kings is in love with you!

He's crazy about you.

He adores you.

You're not a parenthetical thought to Him.

You're *always* on His mind.

He's never *not* thinking about you!

Knowing that is absolute truth . . . shouldn't it affect your life? How you view yourself? How you treat others? How you handle the ordinary details of your everyday happenings?

"I love it when my mom understands what I'm talking about and doesn't judge me."
—Nicole, 15

Shouldn't it affect your concept of God? Knowing—*really knowing* and accepting that He loves you with an everlasting, covenant, eternal, never-ending love—doesn't that make you want to love Him back?

One who loves you enough to bleed for you
and die for you
and conquer death for you
and empower you daily
is certainly One worth serving, obeying, and loving.

You are not a parenthetical thought to God! You're the apple of His eye. You are the reason He created the world. You're His delight. You're why He looks forward to eternity.

You are the reason for covenant.

Yes, God has made a holy covenant with *you*. (We'll get to that later.)

When God thinks about you, He doesn't focus on your weakness, your handicap, or your past. He doesn't use your imperfection to label or identify or define you. He doesn't define Abbie as the one who struggles with an eating disorder. He defines Abbie as His delight, all the while knowing she's throwing up, obsessing over calories in the communion wafer at church, and hurting beyond words. He doesn't identify her with her handicap. He identifies her with himself.

If Abbie has a relationship with Jesus, God sees part of His very self inside of Abbie. Because He's made an eternal covenant with His precious daughter, He pursues her with an unending love; with an intensely focused passion to bring wholeness to her and completeness with Him.

The Reason for Mephibosheth's Handicap

When Mephibosheth's nurse heard the news that David had taken the throne, her motherly instincts kicked into action. She grabbed the little five-year-old and ran. And with good reason.

You see, she knew that whoever succeeded Saul as king (if he was not a member of Saul's family) would probably follow the age-old tradition of killing the former king's family members. This was done to ensure that there wouldn't be an uprising from the former ruler's family.

But Mephibosheth's nurse didn't know David. She wasn't aware of his tender heart or of his holy covenant with Jonathan. All she could see was the immediate. And when you're absorbed in the immediate, you fail to see God working in the extraordinary way He often does behind the scenes.

If David was planning on fulfilling the tradition, Mephibosheth would have topped the list of those to be killed. In the nurse's haste, Mephibosheth fell from her arms and permanently damaged both of his feet. For the rest of his life, he would be crippled.

He would live with a handicap.

His weakness would be highlighted.

It would even define him.

His identity would be wrapped up in the fact that he couldn't walk.

Hmmm.

Have you found your place in this story? Have you played this role? You are the heir of the King of Kings! Yet you've lived with the handicap of sin. Are you allowing it to define you? Or have you accepted healing, forgiveness, wholeness from your Creator?

Do you realize that when you were unable to help yourself, Christ stepped in as part of God's covenant to you? (See Romans 5:6.) God didn't wait until you'd had surgery, been cleaned up, or gone through counseling. He loved you and gave His Son's life for you while you were saturated in sin. *That's*

> "My mom got upset because I had my head on a guy friend's shoulder. We talked for a long time, and I finally showed her that my intentions were pure and promised to use better judgment in the future."
> —Abbie, 16

when He showed His great love for you!
Again . . . what a God!
That's a God worth serving.
That's a God worth loving.
That's a God worthy of our trust.

Meanwhile, Back at the Ranch

With David on the throne, Israel flourished. His success was unmatched. Israel grew ten times in size. They were at peace. People loved their king. But David, the successful king, remembered the sacred covenant he'd made to Jonathan nearly twenty years earlier.

In 2 Samuel 9, we read that David is informed about Mephibosheth.

*David asked, "Is there anyone still left of the house of Saul
to whom I can show kindness for Jonathan's sake?"*

*Now there was a servant of Saul's household named Ziba.
They called him to appear before David, and the king
said to him, "Are you Ziba?"*

"Your servant," he replied.

*The king asked, "Is there no one still left of the house of Saul
to whom I can show God's kindness?" (vv. 1-2)*

The Hebrew word for kindness here is *chesed*. It means a love that will never let go. Think of playing tug-of-war with a Rottweiler. He won't let go! He tenaciously holds the rope in the everlasting grip of his enormous strength. Now multiply that by a zillion and you'll have a hint at the depth of *chesed*. Because of David's holy covenant with Jonathan, he was committed to loving Jonathan's family with a tenacity that would never let go.

Ziba answered the king, "There is still a son of Jonathan;
he is crippled in both feet" (v. 3).

Again . . . notice how Mephibosheth is described. He's defined by his handicap. But that doesn't stop David.

"Where is he?" the king asked.

Ziba answered, "He is at the house of Makir
son of Ammiel in Lo Debar."

So King David had him brought from Lo Debar,
from the house of Makir son of Ammiel. (vv. 4-5)

> *"I love it when my mom talks with me about life and boys and stuff."*
>
> —Jenna, 13

You can imagine the fear Mephibosheth must have felt when he heard the king had summoned him to the palace. *After twenty years, would he now choose to slay me?* he must have wondered.

Knowing that Mephibosheth was crippled, that he would never have anything of significance to offer the kingdom, and knowing he was living in Lo Debar—meaning "a dry and parched land," a place where people were deprived and lived in fear—would have been reason for many in royal places to rationalize rejecting Mephibosheth.

But because of the holy covenant David had made with Jonathan, Mephibosheth's life was about to change forever!

Can you relate?

Have you ever lived in fear?

Have you known what it's like to be deprived?

To have your handicap or weakness made public?

Many kings would quickly cut you off. But because of a holy covenant God made with His Son, Jesus, and with *you* . . . He invites you into the kingdom!

Jesus Does for You . . .

What King David did for Mephibosheth, your heavenly Father does for you! A crippled, lonely woman who knows the reality of living in a spiritually dry place can't see the truth of who she really is. Let Christ remind you of who you are right now:

You are an heir to the kingdom!

You are the apple of His eye.

You are the reason He willingly gave His life.

You are the one who will live in the forever home He's constructing for you right now in His perfect paradise.

Jesus continually looks at the scars on His wrist—the proof of His covenant with His Father and with you— and He asks, "Is there anyone still out there who doesn't know about my covenant? Holy Spirit, go find her! Invite her to the kingdom. I want her at my royal table forever."

"I love it when my mom talks to me honestly about herself."

—Fran, 18

When Ziba informed King David of Mephibosheth, he asked where he was. In the NIV, it simply says, "Where is he?" But in some versions, David says, "Where is this son?"

He called Mephibosheth a son! Even though he's parenthesized in Scripture and referred to as a cripple, David thought of him as a son. He looked past his weakness and saw the power of the covenant shining through.

David's servants made the journey to Lo Debar and carried Mephibosheth inside a chariot to the palace. Imagine his fear as he was taken right into the throne room of the king.

Mephibosheth was scared to death! He bowed low before King David. Let's look at the Scripture:

When Mephibosheth son of Jonathan, the son of Saul, came to David, he bowed down to pay him honor.

David said, "Mephibosheth!"

It must have felt good to be called by his name instead of being referred to by his handicap. Just as David didn't focus on the size of a giant years earlier, he wasn't focusing on the weakness of the one who now bowed in front of him. He called him by his name— giving him dignity. The king showing respect to the reject!

"Your servant," he replied.

He must have been shaking. Quivering. His fear must have been all too obvious, because of David's response:

"I love it when my mom truthfully tells me about her day.
—Natasha, 17

"Don't be afraid," David said to him, "for I will surely show you kindness for the sake of your father Jonathan. I will restore to you all the land that belonged to your grandfather Saul, and you will always eat at my table."

What intimacy! The king inviting the reject . . . to the royal table . . . for royal dining . . . for the rest of his life!

Mephibosheth bowed down and said, "What is your servant, that you should notice a dead dog like me?" (2 Samuel 9:6–8).

Dogs were equated with garbage in those days. Mephibosheth saw himself as trash. Useless. Good for nothing.

But the king saw past his handicap and saw him for who he really was—an heir of royalty!

Have you been there? So down on yourself that you couldn't see your potential? So focused on your weakness that you failed to notice your God-given gifts?

Your King sees past all that.

He knows the truth about you.

And He wants you to know it too: You are an heir of royalty.

Not because of who you are, but because of a holy covenant made between God, His Son, and you!

It Gets Better

Just as King David told Mephibosheth not to be afraid, you'll hear the same words spoken by your King if you listen carefully.

"Don't be afraid!"

"Fear not!"

These are the most repeated words from the mouth of Christ. Four hundred fifty times He tells us not to be afraid. It's in every book of the Bible. Are you listening?

> *"I love it when my mom tucks me in at night and asks me how my day went."*
> —Brandi, 17

Mephibosheth bowed low; he fell to the ground. His actions demonstrated total submission. He was saying, "I'm yours. I'm part of your family now."

What enabled him to do that?

The power of a covenant made twenty years earlier.

And because of that covenant, Mephibosheth's life would now change forever. From that day on, he ate every day with the king and all the royalty of the kingdom. He moved inside the palace. The throne of royalty became his home!

And King David kept his word. He returned to Mephibosheth all the land, crops, and servants that were rightfully his. Mephibosheth lived as royalty the rest of his life. He was in the king's presence, at the king's table every single night.

What About You?

You are an heir of royalty! *You are a daughter of the King of Kings!* Are you experiencing the intimacy of being at His table on a daily basis?

All of us, like Mephibosheth, are handicapped. What's crippling you?

Jealousy?

Insecurity?

Pornography?

An eating disorder?

Lying?

God sees right through your handicap to what you *can* be! He sees beyond the crippling effect of what's holding you back from experiencing wholeness, completeness, royalty!

"I love it when my mom smiles and tells me I did a good job."
—Mandi, 17

He has chosen *you* to sit at His table every single day, to enjoy great intimacy with the King, to live in His holy presence 24/7.

Go ahead.

Pack your baggage.

Time to move into the palace.

You can't make it your home, though, until you leave the baggage at the door. You see, you're an heir of royalty. A daughter of the King. Your baggage doesn't belong in the kingdom. He doesn't want your baggage to weigh you down any longer. He wants to clothe you in royal garb. To dine with you in holy intimacy. He wants you to make His palace your *home*.

Not because you're good enough. You know better.

Not because you deserve it. You don't.

But because of a covenant made with an everlasting love between your King, His Son . . . and *you*.

Think About It

• What's crippling you from becoming all that God wants you to be?

• Are you enjoying the intimacy of being in the King's presence every single day? Dining at His table? Soaking up His Word? If not . . . what's keeping you from it?

• Are you so busy focusing on the giants in your life that you're not seeing the resources God wants to equip you with to face them? What giants are you fighting?

CHAPTER 5

The Types of Covenant

There is so much to teach, and the time goes so fast.
—Erma Bombeck

Okay.

We've talked about the power that a holy covenant had on Mephibosheth and how it changed his life forever. But God has made a holy covenant with you that should change *your* life forever too.

When you understand . . . when you truly get it . . . the meaning and power of this covenant will affect the way you live, the way you carry yourself, the way you interact with others, and the way you see yourself.

Let's do a quick recap of how we defined *covenant* in the first chapter:

A covenant is much more than a decision
promise
commitment
pledge
or agreement.

"I love it when my mom shows that she's interested in my life."
—Ashley, 19

It's even more than a contract. A contract always has an ending date. A covenant never expires. A contract usually involves one part of a person—a specific skill, a certain job to be done, an agreed-upon amount of money. But a covenant involves the totality of a person—his or her total being.

Covenants of God

*He remembers his covenant forever, the word he commanded, for a
thousand generations, the covenant he made with Abraham, the oath
he swore to Isaac. He confirmed it to Jacob as a decree, to Israel as an
everlasting covenant: "To you I will give the land of Canaan as the
portion you will inherit" (Psalm 105:8–11).*

Here are two different types of covenants used in the Old
Testament:

1. Parity Covenant: A covenant between *equal* parties. Both
people voluntarily accepted the terms of the agreement (1 Samuel
18:3–4; Malachi 2:14; Obadiah 7).

2. Suzerain Covenant: A covenant where one of the parties is
superior to another (Ezekiel 17:13–14). In this, God commands a
covenant that man, the servant, is to obey (Joshua 23:16).

Let's take a quick look at a variety of covenants made by God.

- **The Edenic Covenant:** God's promise of redemption (Genesis
  3:15).
- **The Noachian Covenant:** For the preservation of the race
  (Genesis 9:9).
- **The Abrahamic Covenant:** Granting blessings through Abram's
  family (Genesis 15:18).
- **The Sinaitic Covenant:** Designating Israel as God's chosen
  people (Exodus 19:5–6).
- **The Levitical Covenant:** Making reconciliation through priestly
  atonement (Numbers 25:12–13).
- **The Davidic Covenant:** Messianic salvation promised through
  David's dynasty (2 Samuel 23:5).
- **The New Covenant:** Jesus Christ, God's Son, willingly gives His
  life and sheds His blood to enter into a covenant with all humanity (Matthew 26:28).

Wrapped inside these covenants were activities that helped define and seal the covenant. Most covenants were made with cutting and with the exchanging of a variety of items.

"My mom doesn't like how I listen to sad music when I'm sad. Our compromise is that I can listen to sad music in my room and happy music throughout the whole house."

—Fiona, 15

Jonathan took off the robe he was wearing and gave it to David, along with his tunic, and even his sword, his bow and his belt. (1 Samuel 18:4)

Let's take an inside look at some of the details in the above covenants:

1. *Exchange of Robes* (outer garments). This was an exchange of identity. "I am part you, and you are part me. I am no longer focused on my own identity. I take your identity with my own."
2. *Exchange of Belts* (this is where military gear was hung). It symbolized an exchange of strength or assets. "Everything I bring into this relationship is now yours."
3. *Exchange of Weapons.* This was an exchange of enemies, saying essentially, "If anyone comes after you, he'll have to get by me first." The purpose was to protect each other.
4. *The Sacrifice* (to "cut" the animals). A heifer was laid on its back and sliced down the underside of its belly, legs folded out. This is known as a blood covenant. A life must be given or sacrificed. Blood must be shed.
5. *The Walk of Death.* The animal lay cut open between the two people. The partners stood facing each other in an open field so they could be witnessed by others. They would walk through the mass of blood in a figure eight. The number eight was chosen

because it stands for infinity; there is no end; it's an all-connected number.

6. *The Mark of the Body.* This was also known as the striking of hands. The two people made an incision on their wrists and put their forearms together, mingling their blood. They would then wave their hands, revealing the covenant marks to others and letting witnesses know that a covenant has been made.

7. *The Pronouncement of Blessings and Cursings.* As long as you keep the terms of this covenant, you shall experience blessings; if you break the covenant, you'll experience cursings. (See Deuteronomy 28.)

8. *The Covenant Meal.* The two would sit at a table before witnesses and share a meal, feeding the covenant partner first. "As you are ingesting this food, you are ingesting me."

"I love it when my mom holds my hand."
—Mallory, 14

9. *The Exchange of Names.* Each covenant partner took the other's name as a middle name. "I'll take your name in the middle of mine. Every time the new name is pronounced, it tells who my covenant partner is."

So . . .

God has made a "cut covenant" with you! He has cut himself—through His Son, Jesus Christ—and His covenant blood forgives and erases your sins. His covenant grace provides inner strength to handle our hurts. His covenant love is unconditional and unending. His covenant power energizes us to cope and change our lives for the good. His covenant hope guarantees us a future, now and forever!

God has taken the initiative to reach out to you and enter into an eternal love relationship with you. He wants you to know Him. To enjoy holy intimacy with Him. To be His royal heir; to sit at His dining table each night. He wants to be in covenant with you!

Think of It This Way

When God thought up the covenant process, it was as if He was saying, "I will bind myself to Susie, and I'll ask her to bind herself to me. And in doing that, everything I have will be hers. I'll not only offer this covenant to Susie; I'll offer a covenant to all of humanity!"

Abraham understood the concept of covenant. He understood that when one made a covenant, it involved *everything* he had. Why would Almighty God want to share everything He has with Abraham? With Susie? *With you?*

Because He loves us.

And He loves us enough not to ever go back on His word. Maybe like Mephibosheth, you find yourself quivering before the Lord. Listen closely, and you'll hear Him say, "Fear not!"

But we know we're crippled. We're undeserving. We shouldn't be living in the palace with the King of Kings!

Listen closely to the voice of the Father: "I want to love you. Leave Lo Debar. Enter into my holy kingdom. I want you to share my banquet table. According to the covenant I've made through my Son, Jesus, what's mine is now yours."

Gasp.

Are you getting it?

> "I love it when my mom does something crazy with me such as staying up late or eating lots of chocolate."
>
> —Cassandra, 14

God wants to give you His holiness, His riches, His power through Jesus Christ. He never intended for you to live in Lo Debar. He never wanted you to be crippled by what you can't do. He wants to empower you to become holy, to defeat the giants, to live as a royal heir. You're a daughter of the King!

Are You Ready?

The greatest gift you can give your daughter is to be a genuine Christian who reflects Christ in your relationship with her. God through Jesus has a cut covenant with you. By the Holy Spirit in you, He can energize and equip you to keep a holy covenant with your daughter or with your mom.

Mom, because God through Christ has made an eternal, holy covenant with you, He wants you to make a sacred, eternal covenant with your daughter.

Daughter, because God through Christ has made an eternal, holy covenant with you, He wants you to make a sacred, eternal covenant with your mom.

It's a strand of three cords: (1) God through Jesus, (2) mom to daughter, and (3) daughter to mom. If these three strands are woven together to form one holy covenant, your life will change forever! Neither of you will ever be the same.

"I love it when my mom shows she genuinely cares about my friends."

—Hailey, 16

Think About It

- Does your lifestyle reflect life in the palace or life in Lo Debar?
- Have you accepted Christ's covenant for you? Have you placed your faith in Him, confessed your sins, and established a growing

relationship with Him? If not, would you consider praying this prayer from your heart?

Dear Jesus,
This covenant information is new to me. Yes, I've heard the term, but I've never fully understood it. I believe making a covenant with you could actually change my life. And Jesus, I'm ready for a change.

I admit I'm a sinner. I'm sorry I've lived in Lo Debar and have let sin cripple me from becoming all you want me to be. Will you forgive me, Jesus?

I believe the Bible is your holy Word. I believe it's true. I believe you died for me so I wouldn't have to pay the death penalty for my sin. Jesus, I don't deserve that kind of love, but I'm extremely grateful for it!

I accept your forgiveness for my sins. I'm placing my faith in you right now. You have initiated a covenant with me. You have offered me your identity and your treasure of holiness and eternal life. I now enter into your holy covenant. I want your identity. I give you all that I am and all I ever hope to be. I give you my skills, my desires, my will, my rights, my future, my family. I give you everything, Jesus! I now belong to you.

Help me to grow in my understanding of this holy, sacred oath. And please strengthen the three strands of my covenant as I make it with another.

> "It was tough when my mom discovered that I was a cutter. She made me go to counseling, and that really ticked me off. But now I'm glad she did, because I'm actually getting better."
> —Mahalia, 14

In your holy name I pray these things.
Amen.

If you prayed that heartfelt prayer, you'll want to get involved in a church, find a ministry, read and study the Bible, talk with your pastor about baptism, and share your faith with others.

CHAPTER 6

The Evolution of Us

A daughter may outgrow your lap,
but she will never outgrow your heart.
—Author Unknown

Now that you understand the biblical meaning and power of a sacred covenant, let's make this holy oath a reality in your own life.

Don't be intimidated by the idea of entering into a covenant with God and your daughter. You may wonder if you really *want* open and honest communication with her. It means *you* have to be open and honest too, and give her *permission* to be honest with you, even when it hurts. Teens have a way of cutting right to the heart of things—no beating around the bush. You'll commit to being a listener, encourager, and safe place, assuring her that she *can* come to you without fear of being embarrassed.

Remember, this is a process that happens over time. You didn't get where you are now overnight.

Let's reminisce for a moment.

It didn't take long after the birth of your first child for sobering reality to hit: You're responsible for the health and well-being of another human life. It's you this little person depends on for her every need—everything from nourishment and clean diapers to protection from germs and the dangers of a very large outside world.

You're handed a beautiful bundle of perfection—no scars and no disappointments.

You held in your arms a brand-new life waiting to be molded. From the moment of delivery it's your responsibility to care for and teach this little one about life, love, God, and eventually how to become independent of you.

You'll not only be your daughter's *first* teacher; you're also the most influential one she'll ever have. It's through your eyes she'll first see the world. Your words, actions, and attitudes will teach her many things that will shape her life forever.

If you view the world as a beautiful place full of exciting new experiences and promise, she'll absorb your love of life and excitement to experience it.

If you view it through skeptical eyes and focus on the hardships and disappointment life can bring, she's more likely to absorb discouragement and feelings of hopelessness.

You'll be teaching her every moment of every day of her life—whether you realize it or not. You'll either parent her intentionally, realizing the sacredness of the responsibility God has given you as her one and only mother, or you'll be overwhelmed by the size of the task and view your role of motherhood as a burdensome and fearful obligation, feeling totally unprepared for the task.

Children are innately trusting. They'll believe anything you say and are impacted not only by what you say but by how you say it.

Take an honest look at the following:

"I love when my mom appreciates my interests, even though they're not hers."
—Cheri, 16

- Your tone: Are you patient and kind? Or are you snappy and sarcastic?
- Your demeanor: Are you calm and in control? Or are you edgy and easily frustrated?
- Your attitude: Are you encouraging and affirming? Or are you critical and controlling?

Mom, your daughter learns from you—her first teacher in life—how to deal with struggle, disappointment, and loss. She's very good at observing your consistency and integrity, and whether or not your walk matches your talk.

Are rules just for children, but parents are exempt?

They learn that from you.

Are you pleasant to your neighbor but talk about her behind her back?

They learn to respect others (or not) from you.

Do you visit the elderly or take a meal to a family who's hurting?

They learn to care for others from you.

You'll either model love and acceptance of others or teach them to be judgmental and critical.

Mothering is a sobering responsibility. Stop right now and ask yourself this question: How am I doing as my daughter's primary teacher and role model?

"I love it when my mom loves me with her actions."

—Donita, 16

The words you speak to your daughter have power—more power than you may realize. Life and death, blessing and cursing are in the power of your tongue.

If you realize you've not done so well in this area, it's not too late for a fresh start. Invite the Holy Spirit to monitor your tongue and set a watch at the door of your mouth.

Apologize for gossiping or bad-mouthing someone if you need to. That's another valuable lesson your daughter will learn from you—the art of asking forgiveness when you've hurt someone.

Got Help?

A wise mom realizes that she's not up to the task on her own. She takes her role seriously and is intentional in her parenting. Don't be afraid to get help and guidance from those who've already walked this path before you and are raising emotionally healthy and happy children of their own.

Go to your knees for wisdom and strength.

Trust the One who created your daughter.

God knows best how to nurture and encourage her to become all He intended her to be.

Ask for His help as you raise her. He's waiting for you to invite Him into this process!

God has trusted you to be involved in His creative work. His plans for your daughter are far beyond your comprehension: She could grow up to be the doctor who will discover the cure for cancer, or she may become the president of a large ministry. As her mother, you have the power to fan the flame of a dream or snuff it out.

"I love it when my mom's voice squeaks when she talks excitedly."

—Toni, 17

Maybe she'll be a missionary who spends her life in a foreign land, teaching children about the saving grace of Jesus. Whoever your daughter becomes, her life will be shaped by many people but most significantly by the woman who gave her life—you, her mom.

Who's the Boss?

We all have to be taught important life lessons. They don't just happen by osmosis. Effectively teaching children to be responsible young adults requires you to take on the mom role that won't make you popular—the role of Mom the Boss.

If you're like me (Kathy), you had visions of what life with your daughter would be like as you rocked her and sang to her in those wonderful newborn days. You dressed her up in cute outfits, put ribbons in her hair, painted her fingernails, and played Barbies together.

As she got older, you taught her to bake, took her shopping, and laughed and spent countless hours together doing "girl stuff."

Now you envision becoming her best friend. You'll be the one she runs to with the exciting news of being asked out on her first date. You'll teach her to cook and sew, and the two of you will love shopping together.

You'll share the unique bond that moms and daughters have. Life with her is going to be so much fun!

> "I love it when my mom highlights my hair."
> —Zoey, 19

But before long, you may realize you have a very strong-minded young lady who isn't fond of shopping and hates bows in her hair. It becomes very clear that with the title of Mother comes the responsibility to shape, discipline, and direct her energy toward appropriate behavior and respect for authority—your authority as the parent first of all.

You've probably been there. You know that with toddlers, this can be a mighty battle of the wills, one that you as the parent better plan on winning!

I remember clearly the day my precious little brown-eyed two-year-old daughter boldly said to me, "You're not the boss of me!" That was the day the line was drawn in the sand, and the hair on the back of my neck stood straight up. This darling little girl was staring me down, daring me to prove her wrong.

I could have replied, "Oh, yes I am!" all day long, but only saying it wouldn't make it true.

I had to teach her that I was the one in charge, not her. It didn't happen overnight, and it didn't happen without many tears—both hers and mine.

Fortunately, I had the good sense to know that we were in for a long-term battle if we didn't get something straight real quick: I was the parent, she was the child.

Parent First, Friend Later

You can look forward to one day being your daughter's friend, but before you can be her friend, you need to be her parent.

God didn't give you the assignment to be your child's friend when you gave birth.

He gave you the assignment of parent.

Your daughter needs you to say no when she gets too close to the hot stove or wants to chase a ball into the street.

She needs you to teach her to be responsible before she can be independent.

When our kids leave the warm, safe environment of home, they're entering unfamiliar territory full of distractions. The stimulation that comes with new-found independence doesn't always promote logic and wise choices, especially when you partner that with raging hormones and adolescent peer pressure.

Your normally responsible daughter can lose all common sense and track of time when she's out with her friends. She can be totally oblivious to the fact that you've been waiting in

"I love it when my mom chases me through the house laughing."

—Carly, 17

the car for thirty minutes when you go pick her up from shopping at the mall with friends.

While your imagination has you scared to death that she's been abducted by a sex offender, she's simply trying on shoes with her friends and is completely unaware of the time.

With independence comes responsibility.

Teaching this basic life lesson early will save you both a lot of frustration and stress. As your daughter learns to be responsible with independence, you can trust her with more.

"My mom and I went through a tough time when she wanted me to wear more modest clothing and I didn't want to. We just kept working on it and finally found some clothes that we both liked."

—Savannah, 16

Mom the Boss-Counselor

As we mentioned earlier, releasing your daughter into the world is a process that you work toward.

She's learning to handle the responsibility of making more of her own choices, and with that will come some heartaches and disappointment.

There comes a time in the mother-daughter relationship when Mom the Boss evolves into Mom the Boss-Counselor. The power of decision is gradually handed over to your daughter, and you step aside to support her decisions rather than dictate them.

Whether she chooses to try out for cheerleading or apply for the yearbook staff isn't necessarily a moral decision. Just because you were a cheerleader doesn't mean she wants to be.

She wants the freedom to make these kinds of personal-interest choices on her own and develop the talents God has given her, but she still needs your input and guidance.

Has she considered the time commitment that each would require?

What are her strengths?

Where is she most likely to succeed?

Your experience and adult perspective can help guide her choices.

When she's overextended herself and ends up sick because she's not getting enough sleep, she needs Mom the Boss-Counselor to step in and help create balance in her life.

She needs her boss-counselor to look out for her best interest when all her friends are going to an R-rated movie on Friday night and she doesn't have the courage to say no.

Teenagers tend to think they're invincible and don't always consider the consequences of their decisions. That's another reason why God gave them parents!

Releasing the power of decision to your teen daughter should be done with a goal in mind. That goal is to equip her to be confident in her ability to make wise choices when she's out from under the protective roof of your home.

"I love it when my mom tries to be cool and is successful."

—Sidney, 16

She'll make some mistakes along the way and will have to face the consequences of her decisions. Mom the Boss-Counselor is close by, though, and is there for guidance and support.

Mom the Counselor-Friend

Hopefully by the time your daughter's graduating from high school and looking toward her future, you have confidence in her ability to make wise decisions. You've done your homework and given her the experience of making decisions for herself for a few years now in preparation for this day.

At this stage of her life, she needs Mom the Counselor-Friend. She's an adult in the eyes of society and has learned to weigh the pros and cons of major decisions. You've learned to step back, allowing her to pursue her dreams, but you're not out of the picture entirely.

She knows you trust her ability to think for herself. She also knows you're there for her—only a phone call away—when she needs your advice.

She knows you pray for her, and that gives her great peace. She can walk with her head high because Mom the Counselor-Friend gives her daughter the freedom to be who God has created her to be. That empowers her with confidence.

You've reached a place of privilege in your relationship with her.

You've watched her become strong on her own, yet you're the one she turns to when life gets overwhelming and she just needs a mom-hug.

You're the one she calls when she's met that perfect guy or needs to talk about an internship she's been offered. It's a great time in your relationship. She needs you, yet she's not dependent on you.

You've worked hard to get to this point, and it's been well worth the wait!

Mom the Friend

By the time your daughter gets out of college or is planning her wedding, your role once again changes. Now you become Mom the Friend. It's been a natural progression.

There are now other people of major influence in her life: She may have a career and a fiancé. She's an adult woman who's taking responsibility for herself and her future.

You've done the work, now you're reaping the benefits of a job well done! You'll always be her mom, but now you're also her friend!

You spend time together to enjoy each other's company. You've graduated from caregiver and disciplinarian to a source of companionship and giver of wisdom.

She calls you to go shopping and go to lunch. Your young-adult daughter has finally discovered how smart you've been all these years! It's as if someone turned on the light, and she now sees you as a real person with a life and talents of your own. Glorious day!

Mom the Grandma!

One day you'll take on another valuable role in her life, that of Grandma to her children.

Does that seem a million years away? It will be here in the blink of an eye. You'll treasure the closeness between you, and the days of teenage rebellion will be a thing of the past.

You'll have been an instrument in the hand of God to nurture and fashion the life of one of His most precious possessions—the little girl He placed in your care.

"I love it when my mom believes in all my dreams—even the ones she doesn't understand."

—Jennifer, 16

She'll now need you to help her raise her own children and will come to you for wisdom and support.

You will be valued as wise beyond measure as she realizes the sacrifices you made as you poured yourself into her. Can there be any greater joy?

Not in a Million Years

Maybe you're in the thick of battle with a disrespectful and rebellious teen daughter, and what you've just read sounds like a fairy tale.

Perhaps you and your daughter don't even have a relationship. Maybe you don't have anything in common. She doesn't talk to you, let alone listen.

When you try to give her advice, you're met with rolled eyes or a blank stare. You might as well be green and have antennae! As far as she's concerned, you live on different planets. The very idea of ever being friends is totally foreign to both of you.

Don't give up.

Pray for her.

Pray for yourself.

Ask God to restore the relationship between the two of you. Sometimes things happen that are out of our control and affect our relationships with our kids—the death of a spouse, a nasty divorce, harmful outside influences, an unexpected move or family tragedy.

"*I love it when my mom snuggles with me.*"
—Stephanie, 15

Remember this: You are and will always be your daughter's only mother. Stay on your knees for her, believing God to hear and answer your prayers. She needs this from you. She depends on you to fight for her but may never say so.

The Bible tells the parable of the lost sheep. The Shepherd left the ninety-nine sheep to go rescue the one who had strayed. He went out through the briars and the thorns, risking his life for that one that was so precious to him.

Your daughter is more precious t [[**Susie & Kathy: There appears to be text missing here.**]]

He knows where she is and what she's about. He loves her even more than you do.

He thought her up in the first place!

She's one of His creations.

His heart breaks over her waywardness just as yours does.

Partner with God on her behalf. Lift your requests to Him continually. Relinquish her to His care, believing that He will bring her back to you.

The good news is this: Rebellious phases come and go.

Be there for her.

Don't give up, no matter what she does.

Be the one constant in her life that she knows will never change. If our own mothers give up on us, what hope is there?

Evaluate Your Relationship

Ready for a challenge? Take an honest look at where you are in your relationship with your daughter right now. If she's a preteen, ask yourself these questions:

- How have I done in establishing the role of authority as her parent?
- Does she respect my authority and the boundaries she's been given?
- Do I encourage her confidence by giving her appropriate levels of responsibility?

"When my dad died, my mom and I began fighting. I couldn't open up to her and turned to other female mentors, which made Mom jealous. I went through grief counseling and talked about how to develop more intimate relationships. We've both grown a lot since then. We now discuss calmly and are a lot more forgiving of each other."

—Becca, 22

- Am I giving her too much freedom before she's ready to handle the responsibility?
- Do I need to take back some freedom I may have given her prematurely?

  If she's between the ages of thirteen and fifteen, ask yourself these questions:

- Has she proven herself able to handle the responsibilities I've given her?
- Is she ready for more responsibility?
- How good are we at honest communication with each other?
- Can I trust her judgment?
- Do I affirm her for good judgment often enough?
- Is our relationship what I want it to be? If not, what can I do to help change it?

"I love it when my mom remembers the people I talk about."
—Whitney, 16

If she's an older teen:

- How good am I at letting go and giving her more responsibility in making decisions and facing the consequences?
- Has she proven that she's trustworthy?
- Have I proven myself worthy of her trust?
- How have I done in preparing her to be independent after high school?
- In what areas do I need to improve?

If she's an adult young woman:

- Do I respect her privacy?
- Am I still trying to control her decisions?
- Am I enjoyable for her to be around? Does she want to spend time with me?
- Am I a support or a nag?

• Have I given her the blessing of my confidence in her coupled with unconditional love?

Boiling It Down

You may feel as though you've blown it and wish you'd come across this book years sooner.

Know this: It's never too late to make a fresh start.

It takes courage, but in a healthy relationship, parents acknowledge their mistakes and apologize to their kids from time to time. None of us have traveled this road before, and we all make mistakes. And guess what? Your daughter already knows you're not perfect!

Think back to where it was that you lost communication. What happened to cause the rift between you?

What are you willing to do to restore your relationship? A good place to start is by asking God to help you be the mom your daughter needs.

Restoration may require some huge adjustments in your life. To achieve it, you must be willing to do whatever it takes to make things right. Your future relationship with her may depend on it.

"I love it when my mom helps me organize parties."

—Alissa, 14

Every healthy relationship takes time and effort. Resign from the PTA or quit your full-time job if that's what you need to do.

God will be faithful to meet your needs as you commit your family to Him.

Think About It

• What stage of "evolution" are you and your daughter in right now?

- Do you have realistic expectations of your mother/daughter relationship?
- Do you parent by guilt or affirmation?
- Are you giving your daughter permission to be who God created her to be, or are you trying to make her become what you want her to be?

Dear Father,

Thank you for trusting me with the joy and responsibility of motherhood. I recognize I can't do this job by myself; I need wisdom and patience that only you can give. Help me to know when to be tough and when to be tender. I give my daughter(s) to you.

Amen.

CHAPTER 7

Relational Laundry

*My mother was the most beautiful woman I ever saw. All I am I owe
to my mother. I attribute all my success in life to the moral,
intellectual, and physical education I received from her.*
—George Washington

So far we've talked about mom issues and daughter issues—and
hopefully that's enabling you to take a closer look at yourself—
but remember, the purpose of this book is not only to understand
one another better, but to establish and maintain a lifetime covenant between the two of you. This covenant, once planted,
watered, and consistently blooming, will forever change your
relationship.

But before covenants can actually
be made, we need to deal with some
relational laundry. In other words, we
need to clean out the smelly clothes in
the "I can't walk in here" closet. Let's
make a to-do list for our relational
laundry:

*"My mom and I
never work out our
problems; they just keep
repeating themselves."*
—Gaylene, 20

My Laundry Must Be:

- **looked at**
- **picked up**
- **cleaned up**
- **folded and put away**

Looking at the Laundry

What are the difficult issues between the two of you? There may be some areas of strife of which you're not even aware. They still need to be dealt with. Take this quick quiz to discover any sensitive areas that may need some work.

Mom Quiz

(Answers will vary between true/false and multiple choice.)

1. When my daughter tells me she's going to the library, I know she's really going to the library. _____ True _____ False
2. My daughter knows beyond all doubt that I love her unconditionally. _____ True _____ False
3. My daughter's self-esteem:
   _____ a. is healthy.
   _____ b. is very low.
   _____ c. reflects my own self-esteem.
   _____ d. waivers depending on the circumstances.
4. My daughter trusts me explicitly. _____ True _____ False
5. I can talk with my daughter:
   _____ a. about anything at any time.
   _____ b. only when she's willing.
   _____ c. only about surface-level things.
   _____ d. only about things she's interested in.
6. My daughter has a full understanding of the facts of life. _____ True _____ False
7. If my daughter had a question about the facts of life or sexuality in general:
   _____ a. she'd ask me about it.
   _____ b. she'd probably go to a friend.
   _____ c. she'd seek information from the Internet.
   _____ d. she wouldn't ask anyone; she'd keep the question inside.

8. Regarding gender roles:

  _____ a. my daughter understands and embraces her role as a female.

  _____ b. my daughter rebels against anything feminine.

  _____ c. my daughter is confused in her sexuality.

  _____ d. my daughter is extremely uncomfortable with this subject.

9. I understand and embrace my role as a female from a biblical viewpoint.

  _____ True _____ False

10. I consciously make an effort to help my daughter understand her femininity from God's view.

  _____ True _____ False

11. My relationship with Christ:

  _____ a. is solid and growing.

  _____ b. often waivers.

  _____ c. is nonexistent.

  _____ d. is extremely private.

12. I realize that my relationship with Christ affects my daughter.

  _____ True _____ False

13. My daughter views God:

  _____ a. as her best Friend and Savior.

  _____ b. as Someone to think about in church.

  _____ c. as a hateful and cruel ruler.

  _____ d. with mixed feelings.

14. For my daughter to develop a tightly knit, growing relationship with Christ:

  _____ a. she'd need to see it displayed in my own life.

  _____ b. she'd need to get plugged into a church, youth group,

"I love it when my mom takes me places without my sisters, praises me, appreciates the everyday chores I do, and shows that she trusts me."

—Sara, 17

or Bible study.

_____ c. she'd need to realize that He truly is the answer to the void in her life.

_____ d. she'd just need to "keep on keeping on"; she already has a tightly knit, growing relationship with Him.

15. If my daughter were to honestly relay how she feels about me:

_____ a. she'd express love and gratitude.

_____ b. she'd say she loves me, but she'd also say we often disagree about things.

_____ c. she'd admit that she's angry with me and resentful toward me.

_____ d. she probably wouldn't admit there are issues that we need to deal with.

16. When I'm upset with my daughter, I let her know.

_____ True _____ False

17. When my daughter is upset with me:

_____ a. we talk it out.

_____ b. she admits there's a problem, but she distances herself and refuses to talk.

_____ c. she denies a problem even exists and keeps her feelings inside.

_____ d. she verbally expresses her anger.

"I love it when my mom gives me space when I need it."

—Amber, 15

18. The times my daughter and I have fun:

_____ a. are filled with laughter and camaraderie.

_____ b. rarely happen.

_____ c. are usually when we're doing something that benefits her (shopping, etc.).

_____ d. are extremely limited because of my time schedule or _____ (other).

19. My daughter knows she can come to me about anything.
    _____ True _____ False
20. I pray with my daughter:
    _____ a. often.
    _____ b. very rarely.
    _____ c. if there's a need.
    _____ d. hardly ever; but I pray *for* her.

Mom, did you discover any areas that need a little help? Now that we've *looked* at some of your relationship laundry, let's take a peek at *picking up* the laundry. (*Go to page 100.*)

Daughter Quiz

(Answers will vary between true/false and multiple choice.)

1. I'm honest with my mom:
   _____ a. all the time.
   _____ b. most of the time.
   _____ c. once in a while.
   _____ d. only when I know my honesty won't get me in trouble.
2. I tell my mom at least twice a week that I love her.
   _____ True _____ False
3. My mom's self-esteem:
   _____ a. is healthy.
   _____ b. is very low.
   _____ c. influences my own self-esteem.
   _____ d. waivers depending on the circumstances.
4. I trust Mom explicitly.
   _____ True _____ False
5. I can talk with my mom:

"I love it when my mom just listens."

—Kara, 17

_____ a. about anything at any time.

_____ b. only during the times she's not too busy.

_____ c. only about surface-level things.

_____ d. if I act like I have a crisis.

6. If I have a question about the facts of life, or sexuality in general, I'll go to my mom.

_____ True _____ False

7. My mom helps me understand and embrace my role as a female. _____ True _____ False

8. Sometimes I hate my body or have questions about myself. During these times:

_____ a. I talk with Mom about it.

_____ b. I talk with friends.

_____ c. I just stay confused and don't talk with anyone.

_____ d. I yearn to talk with someone but don't know whom to go to.

9. I understand and embrace my role as a female from a biblical viewpoint. _____ True _____ False

10. My mom and I often pray together. _____ True _____ False

11. My relationship with Christ:

_____ a. is solid and growing.

_____ b. often waivers.

_____ c. is nonexistent.

_____ d. is extremely private.

12. My mom's relationship with Christ:

_____ a. is solid and growing.

_____ b. often waivers.

_____ c. is nonexistent.

_____ d. is extremely private.

13. I view God:

_____ a. as my best Friend and Savior.

_____ b. as Someone to think about in church.

_____ c. as a hateful and cruel ruler.

_____ d. with mixed feelings.

14. For my mom and me to grow together spiritually:

   _____ a. we'd need to first grow closer to Christ.

   _____ b. we'd need to get plugged into a church.

   _____ c. we'd need to start reading the Bible, praying together, and discussing spiritual things.

   _____ d. we'd have to both *want* to grow spiritually.

15. If my mom were to honestly relay how she feels about me:

   _____ a. she'd express love and gratitude.

   _____ b. she'd say she loves me, but she'd also say we often disagree about things.

   _____ c. she'd say she loves me, because that sounds good, but I'm not sure I'd really believe her.

   _____ d. she'd say she regrets having me.

"I love it when my mom makes me laugh when I'm mad or sad."

—Megan, 18

16. When I'm upset with my mom, I let her know.

   _____ True _____ False

17. When my mom is upset with me:

   _____ a. we talk it out.

   _____ b. she admits there's a problem, but she distances herself and refuses to talk.

   _____ c. she denies a problem even exists and keeps her feelings inside.

   _____ d. she verbally expresses her anger.

18. The times my mom and I have fun:

   _____ a. are filled with laughter and camaraderie.

_____ b. rarely happen.

_____ c. usually happen when we're doing something she has to do anyway (shopping for work, work-related errands that she includes me in, etc.).

_____ d. are extremely limited because of her time schedule or _____ (other).

19. I wish I could talk to my mom about anything and know she wouldn't get mad. _____ True _____ False

20. I pray for my mom:

_____ a. often.

_____ b. very rarely.

_____ c. if there's a need.

_____ d. when I think about it.

> *"I love it when my mom makes dinner and when she cleans up after me."*
>
> —Abigail, 18

Girls, did you discover any areas that need a little help? Now that we've *looked* at some of your relationship laundry, let's take a peek at *picking up* the laundry.

Picking Up the Laundry

To "pick up" the laundry, we first need to "own" it. After taking the quiz, can you admit there are some dirty pieces of laundry in your relationship? Any covenant between a mom and daughter will be destined to fail if one person is in denial about what she's done or hasn't done and isn't taking responsibility to make it right. Let's look at what can happen when the relational laundry isn't picked up.

I (Susie) met Haley on a two-week *Brio* missions trip to Ecuador. Through broken sobs she shared how unloved and unwanted she felt. When I asked her to go a little deeper, she explained. "When I was just a toddler, my dad began to abuse me. My mom didn't realize what was happening until I was around six. Her solution was to leave my dad in the United States and move the two of us to Canada.

"Even though I was young, I sensed her anger toward me. That became more and more apparent as she slowly voiced the fact that she blamed everything on me. A few years later she remarried, and that man also abused me. I've also been abused by my uncle and stepbrother. For the last several years, Mom has told me again and again that she wishes I'd never been born. She often tells me that she should have had an abortion instead of giving birth to me."

Was it any wonder that Haley felt used? Every significant male in her life had abused her. And isn't it obvious why she would feel alone after hearing her mother's rejection for several years?

> *"I used to yell at my mom a lot, but she talked to me about it and helped me realize what I was becoming. I realized I was being a jerk and asked her to forgive me."*
>
> —Cheyenne, 18

We simply held Haley for about half an hour and just let her weep. Gradually, we were able to help her see that none of the things that had happened to her were her fault. We prayed with her and asked God to begin the healing process that she so desperately needed.

By the end of the trip, Haley had an entirely different countenance.

No, the hurt hadn't magically disappeared, but she was in the process of being healed by the Great Physician.

She was learning to see herself through God's eyes instead of through the eyes of men and her mother.

But first, Haley needed to "pick up" her laundry. She needed to admit there was a problem. Once she began to own the fact that she had been hurt, abused, and rejected, she was able to experience healing.

Are there some pieces of relational laundry you need to pick up?

Is there an eating disorder hidden in a bottom drawer?

A cutting issue underneath the bed?

What about lying, mistrust, drinking, gossip, or other laundry? Will you determine to take ownership of the laundry, pick it up, and deal with it? But I don't know how! you may be thinking.

The how process begins with the what. In other words, instead of feeling overwhelmed, start with simply noticing the laundry.

"Yes, I see it. I see some relational laundry. I'm looking at it." Great. That's a huge start! Now move to the next step of picking it up; owning it.

"Yes, I can see how telling my daughter she needs to lose weight contributed to her eating disorder." Or "I admit that my constant bickering with my husband has caused my daughter to withdraw."

If you'll own the laundry that's yours, we can move to the next step.

"I disobeyed and used my cell phone to call a guy. My mom let me know that she disobeyed and called a guy when she was my age. It was still wrong, but we talked it through and she helped me understand that I can resist temptation with God's help."

—Samantha, 17

Cleaning Up the Laundry

To clean up the relational laundry between you means you're not only willing to forgive and extend grace; it also means you're willing to *seek* forgiveness. What *is* grace?

It's unmerited favor.

Undeserved acceptance.

It's what God offers you each time you blow it. Will you, then, in turn be grace-conscious and extend forgiveness and favor to those around you?

Even those who don't deserve it?

Even those who don't ask for it or even care about receiving it?

Even those who have hurt you so deeply, your wounds still bleed fresh pain almost daily?

That's the key.

Unmerited. Undeserved. Yet forgiven.

"I love it when my mom wakes me up nicely in the morning by telling me how special I am."

—Dana, 17

Samantha's Pain

Seventeen-year-old Samantha told me she had been a sex addict for two years. She'd been introduced to pornography through the Internet. She'd lied to her parents and had distanced herself from the family in order to keep her cybersex activity a secret.

"It began to consume me," she says. "I thought porn was a guy's problem, but it's not. It started slowly at first—just viewing some stuff on the Internet. Then I started going into chat rooms, and it just exploded from there.

"The whole time I had to lie to my folks, because I didn't want them knowing what was going on. I'd never been so deceitful in my life."

I first encouraged Samantha to seek God's forgiveness and give Him total control of her problem. She prayed and expressed a sincere desire to give up her addiction and change her behavior. But that wasn't the end. Samantha now needed to be just as honest with her parents. In other words, she needed to clean up her dirty laundry that had become a barrier between her and her folks.

Yes, Samantha's parents were shocked. As missionaries, they felt they had protected their daughter and had taught her that porn was sinful and broke God's heart.

Though Samantha knew this, she still fell into sin's trap. Her folks forgave her and thanked her for finally being honest and admitting the problem. They then worked together to create a safety net on the family computer so Samantha wouldn't fall into the same trap again.

"I thought my parents were getting a divorce. My mom explained that parents often disagree about a lot of things and that marriage takes a ton of work and that they're in it forever. They're going on twenty-six years now. I'm glad we talked."

—Belynda, 18

Debra's Pain

Fifty-three-year-old Debra grieved over her sixteen-year-old daughter's involvement with alcohol. "Amber's really a good girl at heart," she says, "but she's not a leader. And when she's around non-Christian friends, she doesn't take a stand."

Debra and her husband had brought their children up in a

Christian home, and church involvement was big in their family. Though Amber loved going to church and hanging out with teens in the youth group, Debra knew her daughter's spiritual life was nonexistent—or, at best, extremely casual.

"She missed a couple of curfews," Debra says. "We grounded her, and she seemed truly sorry. But as soon as her punishment was over, she was out with the same friends and missing curfew again."

"I love it when my mom lets loose with me."

—Gretchen, 16

Either Debra or her husband always went into Amber's room at night and kissed her good-night. "I recently smelled alcohol on her as I kissed her," Debra says. "I was so disappointed, I started crying. I sat on the edge of her bed and begged her to tell me what was going on."

Amber started crying too, and she relayed to her mom how hard it was for her to take a stand. "I care about my friends," she said. "I know I shouldn't be doing the things they do, but I don't know how not to. I don't want to just quit hanging out with them. I don't even want to drink. I just feel like I have to."

Amber and her mom prayed and agreed that together, with Dad, they'd try to create a plan to help Amber keep from failing.

"It's not that we don't have a good relationship," Debra says, "or that Amber is angry and withdrawn. She's just involved in the wrong things."

They tried different strategies: appointments with their pastor, professional counseling, restrictions, refusing to allow Amber to hang out with certain friends. Debra and her husband continued to love their daughter and set firm boundaries for her.

"You know what really made the difference?" Debra asks. "It was regarding spring break. Amber's friends had made plans to spend the week unsupervised at an out-of-town beach. Of course, Amber wanted to go!

" 'Everyone else has already purchased their airline tickets,' she told us. She really begged, but we couldn't allow her to participate in a trip with non-Christian friends who would have no adult supervision," Debra says.

"We talked about her vulnerability as a follower, and she even admitted that if she went, it would be extremely difficult for her not to join in the activities her friends would be doing. We continued to affirm our love for her and explained that it wasn't that we wanted to drain the fun out of her life, but that she needed to start making wise choices and find friends who supported her standards.

"Amber has had a lifelong dream to visit Holland. You can imagine her surprise when my husband took the three of us out to dinner one evening and presented Amber and me with two airline tickets to Holland for spring break!

"We were able to spend an entire week of uninterrupted time together. We laughed. We cried. We prayed together. Because Amber was completely away from friends and peer pressure, she was able to admit the bad influence they were having on her life. Amber recommitted her life to Christ while we were in Holland. Being on a trip together also helped her realize the fact that her dad and I are on her side!

"Things didn't change immediately when we returned home, but as Amber saturated herself more and more with God's Word, her desire for her non-Christian friends began to lessen. She knows we'll always love her and that we care enough about her to make decisions she won't always be happy with, but they're decisions we know are in her best interests."

Cleaning It Up

Moms, can you see that when a biblical approach to forgiveness is taken, healing can begin? Granting forgiveness and extending grace don't convert into lack of discipline. As in Debra's situation, discipline was still at the center of their family, but affirmation and forgiveness were always available.

Girls, let's look at a situation from a reverse standpoint. I (Susie) met fifteen-year-old Dasha in Moscow, Russia. She's a new Christian and is being discipled by a female adult in her church. Dasha's mom is an alcoholic. Dad isn't in the picture. Dasha often comes home to find her mother passed out from drinking. When she's not drinking, she's gone or with a variety of men. Dasha is basically left to care for herself and her younger sister.

She was invited to a nearby church and recently accepted Christ as her Savior. "Since my conversion," she says, "I've realized I can't hold bitterness toward my mother. I wish we had a real mother-daughter relationship, but we may never have that. Regardless, I must love her with the love of God and forgive her for not being the mother my sister and I so desperately need."

Hopefully, someday Dasha's mom will come to know the Lord and give up alcohol. The ideal situation would be if her mom would actually start to be a mom to her daughters and seek their forgiveness. And though Dasha is praying for her mother's salvation, she's not waiting on her mom to come around before she extends Christ's love and forgiveness to her.

Girls, you may be in a situation similar to Dasha's. Perhaps your mom needs to seek forgiveness from you and own her laundry that has deeply wounded you. Instead of waiting for your mom to come around, will you determine—with God's help—to love and forgive your mom in spite of the hurt?

God can help you forgive Mom, even though she may never seek for-

"I love it when my mom bakes me a cake."

—Leigh, 16

giveness from you. By forgiving her anyway, you're dealing with the dirty laundry that needs to be cleaned so that you can get on with a healthy life and move to the next step.

Folded and Put Away

The true sign of starting over—the real proof of genuine forgiveness—is laying aside the past completely and beginning from a standpoint of trust and appreciation for the other. Cynthia and her husband had reared their son and daughter in a Christian home and were involved in church.

"During Erica's middle school years and most of her high school years, she was extremely involved in youth group, and our younger son loved the children's activities at church. My husband and I taught a young-adult Sunday school class, and we loved our church.

"I love when my mom acts as God's hands to me by giving me a warm, secure hug when tears are in my eyes."
—Brenna, 18

"Our children professed to have a relationship with Christ and truly enjoyed their involvement in Bible quizzing, youth retreats . . . really, everything the church offered! They loved church! In fact, we'd often leave home half an hour before services started just to pick up all the friends Erica brought with her from school."

When Erica entered her senior year of high school, however, things began to change. "It was a slow change at first," Cynthia says. "She stopped showing interest in church and youth group. She stopped reading her Bible, and she was no longer inviting friends to church."

Erica finally told her parents she didn't want to attend church any longer, and she left home after high school graduation, breaking off all contact with her parents. "Our hearts were broken," Cynthia says. "This was our daughter who had been fervently serving the Lord and loving all things related to the church."

A few years passed, and Cynthia and her husband moved to another state and began to pastor a church. Erica had a baby out of wedlock and seemed to be on a downhill path of destruction. "We just kept praying for her," Cynthia says. "She moved to the city where we were living, and we asked the church to reach out to her as well."

After a few years of soul-searching, Erica began to visit the church her parents were pastoring. "I couldn't ignore their love for me," she says. "I mean . . . I had broken their hearts. I had done everything that I knew was wrong. I had turned my back on my family and on God. But my parents and the church just kept loving me!"

One Sunday morning, Erica and her boyfriend went to church, and he asked Christ to become his Savior. "I rededicated my life to the Lord and sought forgiveness from Him and my family," Erica says. She and her boyfriend got married, now have two children, and are active leaders in her parents' church.

I saw Cynthia and Erica—with Erica's newest baby—recently, and I was thrilled with the closeness between them. Erica and her mom laughed, hugged, and were genuine with each other. Cynthia had wisely folded up the past laundry between herself and her daughter and had put it away forever.

"Erica has sought forgiveness," Cynthia says. "We're thrilled she's back in the church and right with the Lord. And we're blessed to have once again the tight relationship we used to have.

"I suppose I could bring up the fact that she broke our hearts, but why would I do that? God has forgiven her, and we've forgiven her as well. The past is over. We placed that in God's hands a long time ago. We're moving forward. He is so faithful!"

Moms . . . daughters . . . can you move forward? Can you agree to *look at* the laundry between you, *pick up* the laundry and admit it's yours, *clean up* the laundry, and finally *fold it and put it away?*

You won't be able to do this on your own.

But the good news is that your heavenly Father is in the laundry business!

He loves doing laundry.

And He'd love to take care of yours.

> *"I love it when my mom listens to my mending stories, makes my bed, gives me unexpected gifts."*
>
> —Ashleigh, 14

Think About It

- Go ahead. Look at the laundry that may be lying between the two of you. Don't ignore it any longer. Refuse to continue stepping around the pile. Acknowledge it's there.
- Pick it up. Claim it. Admit that it's yours.
- Don't leave it dirty. Wash it in God's forgiveness.
- And let your heavenly Father fold it up and put it away forever.

Dear heavenly Father,

Will you help me actually see my laundry? I'm finally willing to take a look at it. I've let it go for far too long. Will you forgive me?

I admit that it's my laundry. It's been easier to try to ignore it than to have to deal with it. But I'm ready now. I can't clean this mess up by myself. I need your help. So I'm placing all my relational laundry in your hands right now.

Thank you for allowing me to do this. Thank you for wanting my laundry. I realize only you can bring true cleansing. Father, I choose to forgive. I give you the hurt and the memories. Take my laundry and put it away. I release ownership of it right now. It's yours, Father.

Thank you so much. Now help me grow in this healing and cleansing process. In your name I pray these things.

Amen.

Sorry About That

A mother's treasure is her daughter.
—Catherine Pulsifer

This is so short, it's not even a real chapter. But it's so important, we couldn't leave it out.

"I love it when my mom plans an entire day just for the two of us."

—Rachel, 17

After finishing the previous chapter, you may have realized that God has brought some specific things to your mind for which you need to apologize.

If so, please take your apology seriously. How *are* you at admitting you've been wrong? Take this quick quiz to test your apology quotient.

1. When I'm wrong,
   _____ a. I'm the first to admit it.
   _____ b. it takes a lot of talking to convince me.
   _____ c. I rarely admit it.
   _____ d. I tend to place the blame on someone else.
2. When someone apologizes to me,
   _____ a. it increases my respect for her.
   _____ b. I view it as a weakness.
   _____ c. I tend to think, *It's about time!*
   _____ d. I'm very uncomfortable.

3. I know someone is sincere when apologizing

_____ a. when her actions aren't repeated.

_____ b. only if she cries.

_____ c. when she uses fancy words.

_____ d. by the tone of her voice.

4. When I need to apologize,

_____ a. I do so sincerely and willingly.

_____ b. the person I've wronged usually has to hint or come right out and ask for an apology.

_____ c. I try to make light of it, joke about it, and hope the need for an apology will simply go away.

_____ d. I struggle greatly.

5. When someone asks me for forgiveness,

_____ a. I know she's sincerely repentant.

_____ b. I think she must have blown it really big!

_____ c. I assume she's being overly dramatic.

_____ d. I grant it.

I (Susie) grew up in a home where Mom and Dad taught my brother and me to apologize by asking, "Will you forgive me?" instead of saying, "I'm sorry." I'm glad they taught me that lesson, because as an adult, there are times I have to ask others to forgive me, and it's much easier because I've been doing it for a lifetime!

"My mom tried to force a relationship between us, but I told her I'd talk to her in my own time. So she stopped, and now we're much closer."

—Rebecca, 14

Think about it: If you're genuinely apologetic about something, show it by your actions and your words. Oftentimes, "I'm sorry" simply isn't enough. "Sorry about that" seems so casual, flippant.

Sorry about what?

Sorry you got caught?

Sorry the other person interpreted you incorrectly?

Sorry what you did was considered wrong?

But when you say, "Will you forgive me?" you're approaching someone in humility and sincerely expressing your sorrow.

When we repent of our sins and ask Christ to forgive us, we're not simply saying, "Sorry about that. Sorry my sins nailed you to the cross. Sorry I broke your heart."

In the Greek language—the language in which the New Testament was originally written—*repent* means to *turn completely away from.*

What we're really saying when we seek God's forgiveness is, "Oh, dear Jesus! I'm so sorry I've sinned against you and have broken your heart. I'm so sorry I've been disobedient. Will you forgive me? I'm turning the opposite direction right now. With your help, I'm going to build accountability and boundaries in my life that will help me never to go down that path again."

That's true repentance.

"My mom wanted me to go to private school, and I didn't want to. It ended up being the best thing in the world for me, and now when I look back on it, I'm so glad she talked me into it."

—Courtney, 18

That's the heart cry of someone who's genuinely seeking for-giveness.

When you apologize to someone—or seek forgiveness from her—hopefully you're not simply spouting words, but you're *turning away from* and *forsaking* the wrong you did.

That's an apology!

Moms, girls, will you ask the Lord right now to bring to your mind anything in your life for which you need to seek forgiveness?

Stuff I Wish I Could Tell My Mom

- *I sometimes look at porn on the computer.*
- *I wish I could stop cussing.*
- *I have a reputation at school for being "easy."*
- *I'm on birth control.*
- *I'm a liar.*
- *Sometimes she's too sensitive.*
- *I'd love to be tucked in at night.*
- *I make myself throw up at least twice a day.*
- *I sometimes feel like I'm a freak.*
- *I'm really not a Christian.*
- *Being alone scares me.*
- *I'm attracted to bad boys.*
- *I really don't like her meatloaf.*

CHAPTER 8

An Honest Walk With God, Please

*A mother is the truest friend we have, when trials, heavy and sudden,
fall upon us; when adversity takes the place of prosperity; when
friends who rejoice with us in our sunshine, desert us when troubles
thicken around us, still will she cling to us, and endeavor by her
kind precepts and counsels to dissipate the clouds of darkness,
and cause peace to return to our hearts.*
—Washington Irving

Now that we've dealt with the dirty relational laundry, let's jump-start a fresh newness with Christ. Forget the plastic-smile Christianity. Determine to leave behind all "faith by appearance" and dive into a genuine relationship with God with the understanding that nothing more will be done for show.

Can we simply strive for a simple yet real faith that admits to human failings, how we're all really at the foot of the cross, and demonstrates how the love of God is now paramount in our lives?

Authenticity, Please!

Sixteen-year-old Alaina was one of six hundred teens in Panama with us on a two-week international missions trip. She broke curfew, she snuck out of her hotel room, she yelled at her team leaders, and she was seething with anger. I (Susie) pulled her aside and tried to have a heart-to-heart with her.

"Alaina, it's obvious you don't want to be here. Why'd you come on this missions trip?"

"My parents signed me up without me knowing about it," she said. "And by the time I found out, it was too late to back out." (Well, it's actually never too late to back out, but I was disappointed to hear that her folks had forged her testimony on the application and stated that she wanted to learn how to lead others to Christ.)

"Alaina, do you have a relationship with Christ?"

"Of course I do, Susie. And you can't convince me I don't! My dad's a pastor."

(Again, I was disappointed in a pastor who would lie on an application to get his teen daughter on a missions trip, but I also realized this parent's desperation to do anything to help his daughter.)

"Alaina, I'm not trying to make you believe you're not a Christian if you are. I'm simply trying to help you take a focused look at what you believe. If you really have a growing relationship with Jesus, why are you breaking the rules, screaming at your leaders, and causing so much trouble? This is obviously not how Christ would act on a missions trip."

> *"I love it when my mom shares deeply with me and tells me stories about when she was my age."*
> —Heather, 16

"You don't understand, Susie!" Her voice continued at an escalated pitch teeming with anger.

"No, I don't. And I can't, unless you talk to me. I want to try to understand, though. Talk to me, Alaina. What's going on?"

"This past year has been horrible! I had to change schools because these girls were really mean to me and spreading rumors about me, and I was sexually abused, and I hate my family, and you don't know anything!"

I expressed my sorrow to Alaina for such a tough year and especially for her sexual abuse.

I tried to explain that she was a victim—that it wasn't her fault, but if she didn't deal with it, it would continue to reveal itself through anger and destructive behavior.

I asked if I could give her a hug; she refused.

I prayed for her.

And then I connected her with the professional counselor we had brought on our trip.

Anger + Denial = One Unhealthy Family

When we returned home, the counselor and I followed up with Alaina. We spoke with her mom and shared that her daughter had mentioned sexual abuse. "She's really hurting," I said. "And she's very angry. Will you consider taking her to counseling?"

Mom was in complete denial. "Alaina's a great girl. Her dad's the pastor of our church, and we have a wonderful family," she said. "Alaina's just going through a tough time. She'll get over it."

"I love it when my mom kisses me."

—Traci, 15

We continued to correspond with the mom until she finally broke off communication with us. She refused to deal with her daughter's problems and pretended that this churchgoing family was living in a radiant relationship with God.

What's going to happen to Alaina if her mom doesn't come to grips with reality?

Alaina's anger and resentment will finally explode, and she'll run away from home. Or she'll seek what she interprets as "love" from the first guy who'll give her any affirmation at all. And she'll enter into a more destructive phase of her life—whether it's an eating disorder, cutting, drinking, drugs, etc.

It would be great if Mom would sit down with her daughter, wrap her in her arms, and say something like, "Honey, I know you don't want to talk about this, but we have to. Please tell me about the sexual abuse you experienced. I'm dying inside because that happened to you! It was a crime, and it needs to be dealt with.

"It's natural for you to be angry and confused and withdrawn, but I want you to know that I love you with all my life, and I'd die for you! Honey, we can't let this nightmare consume you. We need to talk it out, and we need to take it to God. We also need to find you a Christian counselor to talk with—someone who can help you pick up the pieces, someone who deals with this type of tragedy on a regular basis. I'll do whatever it takes to bring healing to you!"

Wow.

Can you imagine the security Alaina would feel?

I'm guessing at that point, she'd probably break down in tears, and in the safety of her mom's arms—knowing that she's loved—she'd share the nightmare she experienced and move toward healing.

Get Real

But because Alaina's mom was more concerned with keeping up a good image and not rocking her husband's ministry, she willingly turned a deaf ear to her daughter's hurt and anger.

> "I love it when my mom loves me through the hard times."
> —Victoria, 16

Please determine to live in authenticity with the Lord. Being a committed Christian doesn't mean you won't experience tragedy, nor does it mean that life will be easy for you. But it *does* mean that

you serve a God who will empower you with strength,
infuse you with comfort,
and saturate you with His love.
And where does Christ do that?

At the foot of the cross.
Will you meet Him there?
That's the place where broken,
humbled,
hurting Christians go.
That's where Jesus was.
But He didn't stay there long.
And He won't leave you there long either.

"I love it when my mom says good-night to me.

—Katie, 18

But it's admitting we need Him, recognizing that we're broken and confused and overwhelmed with life's nightmares, that brings authenticity.

Jesus loves it when you're real with Him! Leave the plastic smiles at the foot of His cross.

"And the God of all grace, who called you to his eternal glory in Christ, after you have suffered a little while, will himself restore you and make you strong, firm and steadfast. To him be the power for ever and ever. Amen" (I Peter 5:10-11).

Stuff Happens

Fourteen-year-old Meredith was in Costa Rica with us. The team was having devotions before loading the bus and heading out for their day of ministry. During prayer time, she raised her hand.

"I have a prayer request," she announced nonchalantly. All eyes turned her way. I (Kathy) nodded for her to continue.

"Three weeks before I came on this missions trip, I was raped," she stated. "He was a youth worker at my church. He was new. We don't even know where he came from. He just showed up at church and started helping with the teens. We had just finished playing softball, and I couldn't reach my mom to come pick me up. So this guy offered to give me a ride.

"I got into his car, and instead of taking me directly home, he pulled into a secluded area and raped me. I didn't tell my mom, because I was afraid she wouldn't let me come on this trip if she found out. But I told my older sister, and she took me to get a pregnancy test. I'm supposed to find out during this trip if I'm pregnant. Please pray that I'm not."

Our team was in shock.

We prayed for her and loaded the bus to involve ourselves for ministry. I sat with Meredith on the bus.

With my arm around this fourteen-year-old's shoulders, I said, "Honey, your mom needs to know. If this had happened to my daughter, I'd want to know. We need to tell her. Will you let me help you talk with her?"

Meredith was hesitant at first, but I continued to talk with her, and she finally agreed. That afternoon, when we returned from ministry, Meredith and I made the phone call to her mom.

"I wanted to hang out with my friends, and my mom thought it was because I didn't want to be with her. I really didn't know she wanted to hang that day, but it took a while for me to convince her. We ended up spending the whole day together and had a blast."

—Gwendlyn, 17

I listened as Meredith shared the tragic crime that had happened to her. Then Meredith handed the phone to me.

"Mrs. Simmons, this is Kathy Gowler. I'm your daughter's team leader. I'm so sorry to hear about this, and we'll do whatever we can to help your daughter."

Meredith's mom expressed no emotion at all. "Well, these things happen, you know." Sigh. "It happened to me when I was a teenager; it's happened to Meredith's older sister. It was bound to happen at some point. I'll take her to a doctor when she gets home, but I'm sure she'll be fine."

My heart dropped.
My mind exploded.
Huh?!

I shared the situation with Susie, who was shocked and simply yelled, "This is ridiculous! And she calls herself a mother? That lady's sick! She's not living in reality! Her daughter needs her!"

After we calmed down only slightly, Susie and I talked about Meredith's situation and our sadness that she would return home and eventually begin to believe that what happened to her was just something that happens to most girls. Our hearts wept for a gal we wanted to see rise above the nightmare.

> *"I love it when my mom makes dinner for our family."*
>
> —Neely, 18

Fresh Start

Meredith's birthday happened to be the following Sunday. My husband and I decided to present her with a True Love Waits ring. We wanted to explain in front of the team that what had happened to Meredith was a crime; it was wrong; it should have *never* happened; it broke God's heart . . . and that she was a victim. God wanted healing for her.

My husband, Jeff, placed the True Love Waits ring on top of our Bible and addressed our team.

"Girls, each one of you is a princess of the King of Kings. God delights in you! He loves you more than you'll ever comprehend. Do you know His heart breaks when something bad happens to you? He weeps *with* you. Psalm 34 tells us that God is very close to the brokenhearted. So *know* that when you're hurting, God hurts with you.

"Meredith, what happened to you wasn't your fault. It was a sick crime committed by a sick man on an innocent young lady. He stole something from you that he had no right to take. But, Meredith, do you know how God sees you? When He looks at you right now, He sees you as His beautiful daughter. He glows with pride for you. He looks deep inside your heart, and He sees a pure, whole young lady. You are pure, Meredith.

"God wants you to save your sexual intimacy until marriage. And today you can reiterate your covenant to do that—just as you were before this happened to you. From this day forward, Meredith, you can be a spiritual virgin, because God still sees you as a precious, innocent, pure virgin.

"I love it when my mom always knows when I need to talk."

—Braelyn, 17

"Meredith, we want to give you this True Love Waits ring on your birthday as a symbol that you are whole in the eyes of God. Will you allow Him to begin the healing that you need?"

There wasn't a dry eye in the group. Not just Meredith—but every girl on our team was powerfully reminded of the importance of being sexually pure in God's eyes. Meredith prayed in front of our group, and she took the ring and placed it on her finger. As she did so, she smiled with the understanding that rape *isn't* something that just happens. She knew what she had experienced was terribly wrong. But she also knew God was beginning to heal the pain and confusion.

Wake Up!

Thankfully, Meredith had godly team leaders who knew the importance of restoring her sexual purity. But how much more meaningful could that have been if her own mother had reclaimed her purity and pointed her to Christ?

Yes, Mom was a Christian.

She went to church.

She wore the plastic smile.

She pretended that all was fine with her family.

But she harbored the secret of rape against herself and her two daughters.

Mom, Jesus invites you to the cross. And He wants you to bring Meredith. Don't you realize that you have the power—as her mom—to help her see that what happened to her was a crime? But instead, you choose to ignore it. You deny that your daughter needs help and hope and healing.

"My mom purposely overdosed last year. There was a lot of anger and bitterness between us. It took lots of prayer and give-and-take both ways to overcome the hurt we both felt."

—Carrie, 20

Genuine Spirituality

So what does it mean to live in spiritual authenticity? It means that you commit 100 percent of your life to His authority. You admit to God and to others when you have a need. You determine to be real, to let Him echo through your life. When you hurt, you share it.

But how's that being a strong Christian? you may be thinking.

It's imitating Christ. Check out Ephesians 5:1: "Therefore be imitators of God" (NKJV). In other words, it's okay—and even expected—to be a spiritual copycat of Christ himself.

And guess what Christ did?

When He was angry, He expressed it. (Remember the money-changers in the temple? See Matthew 21:12–13.)

He wept when He felt sorrow. (At the grave of His friend Lazarus. See John 11:32–35.)

When He knew His disciples needed prayer, He instructed them to seek the Father. (His last night with the Twelve before He was crucified, He specifically instructed them to pray. See Luke 22:39–45.)

When His heart broke, He wept openly. (He was so burdened for the people of Jerusalem, He cried over them. See Luke 19:41.)

When He felt joy, He showed it. (He took little children into His arms. See Mark 10:13–16.)

When He saw a need, He met it. (He brought sight to the blind. See Luke 18:41–42.)

When He was disappointed, He didn't hide it. (He told Peter that His "rock-solid disciple" was sounding like Satan. See Matthew 16:22–23.)

> "When I dated my first boyfriend, Mom knew I wasn't in God's will, but I didn't respect her authority or wisdom. I wish I had."
>
> —Regina, 18

Jesus was *real*.

Genuine.

Authentic.

And He asks you to imitate Him!

So know that it's okay to hurt and cry and need.

Go ahead. Take off the mask. Isn't it starting to feel a little tight anyway? One of the reasons Jesus came was so that you could experience freedom! (See John 8:33.) Imagine how free you'll feel without hiding any longer behind that snug-fitting mask! You can find freedom and authenticity in a totally surrendered relationship with Jesus Christ.

Jesus was vulnerable. Open. Authentic.

He expects the same from you.

Staying Real

And once I've committed to spiritual authenticity, how can I maintain it?

Good question.

I like a story Madeleine L'Engle tells in her book *Walking on Water: Reflections on Faith and Art*. She borrows the story from Lewis Carroll, and I'll borrow it from both of them.

The story is about a small village. A clockmaker and repairer lived there. Whenever a clock, watch, or any timepiece needed repair, he fixed it. Time went on, and eventually the clockmaker died without leaving any children or apprentices to carry on his work.

The various timepieces throughout the village began to break. Because there was no one in the village to fix them, a clock might strike midnight at 2:00 PM and watches would gain and lose time. Eventually the villagers' timepieces had no value because they couldn't keep the correct time.

One day, however, a renowned clockmaker and repairer came through the village. People crowded around him with their broken timepieces and begged him to fix them. He spent much of the week looking at the faulty clocks and watches and finally announced that he would only be able to

"I love it when my mom sings to me and treats me like her best friend and not a kid."

—Emily, 16

repair those whose owners had kept them wound, because they were the only ones that would be able to remember how to keep time.

I like the message this story seems to give: We must keep things wound daily. Pray—even when you don't feel like it. Perhaps you've heard the saying, "When it's hardest to pray, pray the hardest."

Read God's Word even when your schedule is full. Commune with the Lord when you're weary and tired. *Why?* Because as you do, He'll infuse you with strength. He'll saturate you with His love.

"I love it when my mom prays for me."
—Suzanne, 14

The daily practice of keeping "spiritually wound up" will help you maintain spiritual authenticity. Prayer and Bible reading will let you know if you've started to pull the mask back over your face. To live in freedom requires the discipline to maintain that freedom by spending time daily with your Creator.

Think About It

- What have you done recently to make others think everything's okay in your family?
- Have you truly committed everything to the authority of Christ?
- Describe the freedom that can only come when Christ is in total control.

Dear Jesus,

No more pretending. No more plastic smiles. I come right now to the foot of your cross, and I come humbly admitting I need your help. I no longer want to be proud or in denial. I want you in all your fullness.

I surrender all, Father. My self. My will. My relationships. My family. My future. My past. The hurt. The anger. The confusion. I give it all to you. I place it now at the foot of your cross. Will you forgive me, Father, for trying to handle life in my own strength? I admit I'm weak. I need your help.

I want to be like you. I want to imitate your life. I desire your genuineness, your authenticity. Break me, Jesus. And reshape me in YOUR holy image.

In your precious name I ask these things.

Amen.

CHAPTER 9

Ready, Set . . . STOP!

A daughter is a little girl who grows up to be a friend.
—Author Unknown

Before we go any further, stop for a moment and answer the following questions:

• How often do you express your love for one another?

_____

• How do you express your love?

_____

_____

_____

Well-known author Gary Chapman has written about the five languages of love. He says there are five different ways we express our love to others. One person may require a different expression of love than you do. In *The Five Love Languages of Teenagers*, Gary suggests the following ways of expressing love:

1. Words of Affirmation
2. Physical Touch
3. Quality Time
4. Acts of Service
5. Gifts

Moms, when you're given a gift, it may not mean as much to you as it would if that same person would simply spend time with you. It all depends on your love language.

Girls, do you know your mom's love language?

Moms, do you know your daughter's love language?

If time means more than gifts, and you're wrapped up in a spending frenzy trying to show your love, your efforts won't be received as love. So determine to recognize the two most important ways each of you interprets, expresses, and receives love.

"I lied about something to my mom. I knew I had to tell her the truth eventually. It took me four hours in the car to get it out, but our relationship has been much stronger since!"

—Britni, 18

Affirming Words

"I love it when my mom tells me she's proud of me," Tasha says. "It makes me feel valuable. It makes me want to continue to do my best."

"My daughter rarely says anything positive to me," Joan says. "It would mean the world to me if she'd just compliment me once in a while."

Many people need to be loved through verbal affirmation. Grab your pencil; it's time for some participation. (We'll start with writing, then we'll move to verbal affirmation.)

Girls, list some things for which you can affirm your mom. We'll get you started, and you finish the list.

1. You're a good cook.
2. You take good care of our family.

3. _____

4. _____

5. _____

Moms, it's your turn. Take a moment to list some things for which you can affirm your daughter. We'll get you started, and you finish the list.

1. You have a good sense of humor.
2. You put thought and time into what you wear and how you do your hair.

3. _____

4. _____

5. _____

Now STOP!
Close the book.
Put it down.
Look at each other and verbally articulate what you've written. (Then meet us back here when you're done.)

The Power of Touch

We met sixteen-year-old Bethany on our missions trip to Peru. Her team leaders complained that she was critical and questioned almost everything they said. I (Kathy) pulled her aside, looked her in the eye, and asked how I could help.

Bethany began with the same negative outbursts she had given her team leaders. In an effort to diffuse the comments, I reached out to her and gave her a light hug. "I know you're hurting," I said. "And we want to help, but you have to talk to us."

Bethany looked up as tears began to trickle down her cheeks.

> *"I love it when my mom calls me randomly to say she's thinking about me."*
>
> —Hosanna, 21

"Why did you hug me?" she asked.

"Because I want you to know that I care about you," I said.

Through a tearstained voice, Bethany said, "My mom has never hugged me. Ever."

"Your mom has never hugged you?" I repeated.

"My whole life, my mom has never hugged me," Bethany said. I simply held the hurting sixteen-year-old. There was no need to explain why she'd been acting out. *Everyone* needs to be hugged!

> *"I love it when my mom lets me have lots of friends over."*
>
> —Gracie, 16

I then placed my hands on Bethany's shoulders. "For the rest of this trip," I said, "I want you to come find me every day and let me hug you. Do you understand? That's your assignment. Every day you're going to get hugged by me."

Bethany grinned, slightly embarrassed, and nodded her head. Guess what improved? Her behavior. Her relationship with her teammates and team leaders. And sure enough, each day, Bethany found me and announced, "I'm ready for my hug."

Healing Through Touch

Why is touch so important? If it's done in a loving way, it gives us value. We're affirmed by someone's hand on our shoulder. A pat on the back helps us realize we're not alone. A hug says, "I care about you and what you're experiencing."

But is touching always appropriate?

No.

In leader training for our missions trips, we explain the difference between appropriate touch and inappropriate touch. "Guaranteed, we'll have some teen girls on this trip who have never been touched appropriately by a male," I say. "And I'd love for them to learn and experience appropriate touch from a godly male leader during the next two weeks."

We tell our males not to give frontal hugs, but to simply place an arm around the shoulders for a quick squeeze or an appropriate side hug. We encourage all our leaders to make it a priority to touch every single teen in an appropriate way.

In fact, every night we have "tuck-ins" for all the girls. After curfew, when everyone's in their assigned room, the female leaders will split up and go to each room and make time to sit on the edge of the girls' beds, give them a good-night hug, and ask if there's anything they need to pray about.

Our male leaders go into the teen guys' rooms and do what we call a "slap-in." Of course, they're not actually slapping anyone, but each male leader will make an effort to lightheartedly "punch" each guy on the arm or pat him on the back and ask him if he wants to pray about anything specific.

It's during these nighttime routines that our students will often open up with hurts and fears. Why? Simply because of the power of touch. When we're touched by someone who truly cares about us, it gives us the security we need to be open and honest. We feel loved.

"I love it when my mom demands that she needs a hug from me."

—Emma, 18

Always Touch?

Of course, there are times in a teen's life when it's best not to touch her. If she's with a group of her friends, it's probably not the wisest time to pinch her cheeks and tell her how much you love her.

Moms, you can learn to interpret the body language of your

daughter, and that will let you know when she's open to being touched and when she's not.

For example, Sandra knows when her thirteen-year-old daughter Nikki, comes through the door if she's willing to be touched. "She'll start telling me about her day," Sandra says. "Sometimes she'll toss her books on the floor and plop down on the sofa and continue talking while I'm in the other room. I know those are the times she's not especially looking for touch.

"But other times she'll come find me—no matter what room of the house I'm in—and tell me about her day. When she does this—when she comes physically close to me—I know she's saying she wants to be touched."

Girls, can you read your mom's body language? If she's engrossed in the newspaper or diligently working on the computer, she may need some space. But look for times when she's able to handle more than one thing at once. For example, when she's stirring something on the stove for dinner, walk up behind her with a quick "I love you" hug.

As she's putting on her makeup in the morning, stand behind her and rub her shoulders. When she's stretched out on the couch, pick up her feet, place them in your lap, and gently rub them. You'll be shouting volumes without ever saying a word!

> "Mom and I fought all the time. I tried to kill myself, and she was there and showed me how much she truly loved me. I realized how stupid I was being, and we've been very close ever since."
> —Shena, 18

Time Well Spent

Connie didn't feel loved by her fourteen-year-old daughter, Hannah. When asked about it, Hannah was shocked. "Of course I love my mom," she said. "I tell her so every single day!"

But Connie's love language wasn't verbal; it was spending time together. Connie explained, "Yes, Hannah often tells me she loves me, but I feel as though it's just words. Anyone can say, 'I love you.' If she really loves me, why doesn't she spend some quality time with me? I'll only have Hannah at home for four more years. Then she'll leave for college. I just want us to spend time together. Is that too much to ask?"

Hannah was a popular student involved in track, the swim team, and student government. "Wow, I never knew she felt that way," Hannah said. "My schedule is jammed! On Saturdays, I'm trying to do homework, and the other weekdays are filled with school and swim practice in the morning and track in the afternoon."

"I love it when my mom looks at pictures with me from when I was little."

—Kristina, 20

Of course, Connie knew Hannah's schedule and didn't want her daughter to drop out of anything that she was involved in, but she still hurt due to their lack of time together.

After talking it through, they created a plan that worked for both of them. "I'm not a late-night person," Connie said. "I usually go to bed around 9:00 p.m.."

Hannah usually didn't wrap up school responsibilities (studying, homework, etc.) until 10 p.m.. "I decided if I wanted quality time with my daughter, I had to find it on her terms," Connie said. "So I've started reading a book at nine, and at ten, when I know Hannah is getting ready for bed, I head into her room and brush her hair. We talk while she gets ready for bed. Then I just sit on the edge of her bed for about twenty minutes, and we pray together. It's made all the difference in the world!"

Hannah made a few changes as well. "I've started doing more

of my homework during study hall," she says, "so that on Saturday I'm not so crammed with trying to catch up. That leaves time for Mom and me to run errands together."

They're usually not doing anything spectacular on Saturday afternoons. Connie says the two of them get groceries and gas, do a little shopping for Hannah, and head home. "But just that little bit of time together shouts volumes that Hannah means it when she tells me she loves me."

Or . . . the Other Way Around

Moms, it might be just the opposite for you. Perhaps quality time isn't *your* love language, but your daughter may desperately need it. As an administrative assistant, Vicky had her hands full. She usually got home from work around five-thirty and hurried to get dinner started. Because she was involved in several committees at church, her evenings were often spent on the phone or at meetings.

But when Vicky's daughter Dawnelle announced that she had to complete a science project in two weeks, Vicky heard the need and got someone else to temporarily cover her church responsibilities. "My mom's really busy," Dawnelle says. "But when I need help, she's willing to drop everything and give me the time I need. That's how I know she loves me."

Moms, when was the last time you spent quality time with your daughter?

Girls, when was the last time you spent time with your mom?

What did the two of you do together? How did it make you feel?

A Servant's Heart

"How do I know my mom loves me?" Chelsea repeated. "Well, that's easy. When I'm sick, she makes me homemade chicken soup.

She makes a special bed for me on the couch so I can watch TV if I feel like it. And she brings my special blanket to cover me up with."

"What else does your mom do to let you know she loves you?" we asked.

"Well, she always hems my jeans. See, I'm shorter than most girls my age, and I can't ever find jeans that fit my height. So my mom always hems them for me."

It's obvious that Chelsea's love language is service. "If my mom didn't love me, she wouldn't work so hard to provide for me," Chelsea says.

Girls, what if your mom interprets service as love? What are you doing to serve her? Could you clear the table without being asked? What about doing the laundry or cooking a special meal?

"I love it when my mom laughs at me when I'm being silly."
—Hattie, 16

If your mom's love language is serving, anything you do to help her will be interpreted that you're doing it because you love her.

Diane taught Abby to show love through service. "Anytime someone in the church is sick, my mom and I bake bread and deliver it to them," Abby says. "And we also visit people in the hospital and pray for them."

Moms, are there specific ways you can teach your daughter how to cultivate a servant's heart? Whether or not that's her love language, God calls all of us to serve Him by serving others. Are you teaching your daughter this important lesson?

Surprise!

I (Susie) enjoy giving gifts to those I love. When my friend Cheryl—who's a pastor's wife—was going to have the church board over for dinner one night, I left work early to clean the house for her. I knew her hands were full with helping two children with homework and preparing a dinner for fourteen people, so I thought the best thing I could do to help would be to clean her house.

I often send special cards through the mail. I recently sent Cindy a card expressing appreciation for all the behind-the-scenes work she does in our church that often goes unnoticed. I slipped a gift certificate for one of her favorite fast-food restaurants inside.

> "I love it when my mom talks with me about my boyfriend relationships."
> —Janna, 16

It's been several years, but I'll never forget receiving a card from Greg and his wife, who lived in another state. It simply said, "Wish we were having lunch together today. We miss you. So have lunch on us." They included a five-dollar bill inside the envelope. I grinned all day about that!

Everyone enjoys gifts, and many people use gifts as a way to express their love to others. Moms, describe a special gift your daughter has given you.

_____

_____

_____

Girls, what's the most special gift you've ever received from your mom?

_____

_____

_____

An "I love you" gift doesn't have to be extravagant, but it's always more special if it carries a special meaning to the receiver. A few birthdays ago, Kathy really surprised me. I went to my hairdresser for my monthly haircut and style. As I reached inside my purse to pull out my checkbook, Shari said, "No need to pay, Susie. It's already taken care of."

"What are you talking about?" I said.

"Kathy's got you covered," she explained. "She called a few weeks ago asking when your next hair appointment was. I told her it was today. And last night, she drove to my house and paid me in advance for today. She even tipped me! So get out of here!"

Wow. What a fun surprise!

Unexpected.

Undeserved.

But so appreciated.

When I was a little girl, I'd spend hours in our garage "speaking and teaching" to my audience of dolls and stuffed animals. Imagine my surprise when, one Saturday, my dad unveiled a podium he'd made for me! "Here you go, Susie. Now you can speak behind a podium just like a professional speaker."

Wow!

I could hardly contain my excitement. I actually gathered kids from the neighborhood and convinced them to sit on the floor of our garage so I could "teach" them. Ha!

I've always been short and often told my parents how much I wished I could be taller. I was speechless to see the pair of stilts my

"My mom and I fought a lot when I started dating. She didn't want me to date because of the mistakes she made when she was my age. We talked about boundaries and healthy relationships. It really helped!"
—Nikkie, 19

dad made me. "Now you *can* be taller," he said. "Just be very careful!"

What's Your Love Language?

As an adult, I'm still trying to figure out what my specific love language is. I must be really needy, because I thrive on all five types of love languages. I'll always remember the special Valentine heart-shaped cakes my mom helped me make every year on February 13 so I could give them to friends and teachers the next day.

Mom taught elementary school and was surely tired by the time she got home, but she took time to help me create special cakes. She showed me she loved me through service.

And during my high school years, she demonstrated her love for me with quality time spent together. Each Monday, after picking me up from piano lessons, she and I would have dinner together—just the two of us—at an Oklahoma City restaurant called Jolly Roger. (She clipped the coupon out of the paper each week for a buy-one-get-one-free dinner. She was smart too!)

"I love it when my mom lets us eat in front of the TV."
—Katy, 17

And she verbally affirmed me. I'll never forget the Saturday morning during my senior year of high school when she quietly walked into my bedroom and woke me up. "Susie," she said, "I believe God has His hand on your life in a very special way. He's going to use you to bring glory to His name."

Wow.

I believed her. Can you imagine how sacred that moment was for me? Though she probably didn't realize it, Mom was placing a blessing on my life. From that point on, I wanted to live up to the blessing.

Mom died three years ago, but even in my adult years as I'd talk with her and Dad on the phone, they'd always end the conversation with, "We love you, Susie. We're so proud of you." Because of their verbal affirmation, I knew I was loved.

My parents also hugged and kissed me. They helped me become comfortable in showing love through touch. And today, I often find myself reaching out to touch someone on the shoulder or freely giving a hug.

Whatever way you give and receive love most comfortably is probably your specific love language. But I have a sneaking suspicion that many of us may rotate among all the languages of love. So strive to develop words of affirmation for one another. Determine to spend quality time together. Hug and touch appropriately. Serve one another with love. And be daring with a surprise gift once in a while!

"I love it when my mom sends me emails."

—Tasha, 15

Time for Action!

Ready for an assignment? This shouldn't be done quickly. In fact, it may even take you an entire week to complete it. That's okay.

Take this assignment seriously!

This will be the most personal letter you have ever written to another person. This will more than likely be a keepsake both of you will treasure for a lifetime!

So, moms and daughters, grab a pen and some paper (or sit down at the computer) and begin writing a letter to each other. The longer the better.

Talk about your past. Are there areas in which you need to

142 SHELLENBERGER • GOWLER

confess? Apologize? Make right? Affirm?

Then move to the present. Talk about your current relationship with each other. Note the strong areas and the weak areas of your relationship. (Don't use this as a finger-pointing time; use it as a time for healing and affirmation and honesty.)

Next, move to the future. What do you want for your relationship in the coming years? What will you specifically do to make it happen?

Please understand that you can't start the next chapter until this assignment has been completed.

Think About It

"I love it when my mom hugs me really tight."
—Evangeline, 16

- In which area do you most naturally show your love to others? (Words, touch, gifts, time, service.)
- In which area do you most enjoy receiving love?
- Will you strive to develop each type of love language to its fullest potential?

Father,

I admit I often get so carried away with my own responsibilities that I fail to show the ones I love most just how much I love them. Please help me to consciously act out the five love languages. And help me to become more comfortable in receiving love from others.

Amen.

CHAPTER 10

Making a Covenant: For Moms Only

The mother-daughter relationship is the most complex.
—Wynonna Judd

Though we've talked about almost everything from A to Z in this book, our purpose is to help you make a covenant with God and with your daughter. In previous chapters you've had opportunities to make a covenant with God. Now it's time to talk about covenant-making with your daughter.

Moms, there are five parts to the covenant you're being challenged to make with your daughter. The only way you can be successful at making and keeping this sacred oath with her is by first having a covenant with your heavenly Father.

Even though you've had opportunities to do so already, let's be sure you feel grounded spiritually, okay?

"I love it when my mom tells me I've done something right."

—Angelina, 16

1. I've experienced and expressed remorse for my sins. I've repented in sorrow to Christ and have sought His forgiveness.
   _____ True _____ False
2. I believe Christ has forgiven my sins. (See Romans 3:22–24.)
   _____ True _____ False

3. I have placed my faith in Christ and have given Him control of my life. _____ True _____ False
4. I still mess up, but when I do, I ask God to forgive me, and He does. _____ True _____ False
5. I understand that prayer and reading my Bible are necessary ingredients for my spiritual growth. _____ True _____ False
6. I have made a covenant to serve God the rest of my life. _____ True _____ False

Moms, if you couldn't answer true to any of the above statements, will you take the time to make it right before God *now*? If you don't have a genuine covenant with God, you can't have a genuine covenant with your daughter. Is there any spiritual business you need to do with the Lord? Do it now!

Mom's Five-Part Covenant to Her Daughter

Mom: *"I make a sacred covenant with you . . .*
#1: to be a godly role model."
#2: to be here for you; to be your safety net."
#3: to pray for you every day."
#4: to consistently pray with you."
#5: to help you unfold the unique personality and gifts with which you've been blessed."

Let's discuss each facet of this sacred covenant so you'll have a full understanding of what you're promising your daughter.

"I love it when my mom prays with me."
—Candace, 16

#1: *"I make a sacred covenant with you to be a godly role model."*

It's not fair to expect spiritual aspirations of your daughter if you're not being the spiritual example she needs to emulate. The apostle Paul told the early Christians to watch his life and learn from him.

Moms, you too can be that confident in your relationship with Christ. You can be so in love with Jesus that you'll wisely tell your daughter to watch your lifestyle and emulate what she sees. Does that mean you're perfect? No. But you can have a perfect heart without perfect behavior.

Let's take a peek at 1 Peter 1:15–16: "But just as he who called you is holy, so be holy in all you do; for it is written: 'Be holy, because I am holy.'"

We tend to think of holiness in terms of perfection and perfection in terms of behavior. But by being "perfect," God is calling us to become one with Him. He wants to sanctify us, cleanse us from unrighteousness, and empower us to live the godly life He yearns for us to live. He can perfect our hearts as He sanctifies us completely.

"I love it when my mom gives me a new book to read that she liked."

—Lisa, 15

Moms, have you asked the Lord to perfect your heart? To cleanse you and release the power of His Holy Spirit within you? When you do that, you begin to live in His lordship. When His Holy Spirit saturates your life and consumes your being, His thoughts become your thoughts. Your deepest desire is to live in the center of His will. You fall so in love with Christ that you yearn to be in His presence 24/7.

You'll never be perfect in behavior until you get to heaven, but God can perfect your heart in such a way that you truly want His will over your own will and relinquish your rights to His authority.

Does this mean you'll never mess up? No. God won't transform your humanity until you get to heaven. While you're on earth, you're still human, and you'll still have human emotions and make mistakes. But the difference is found in your heart. Your motive, your desire, your yearning is to do the will of God.

So when you *do* mess up, you simply seek your Father with genuine repentance (meaning you're not only sorry for your sin, but you're also turning away from it), and He is faithful to forgive. That's not weakness, it's spiritual growth!

And the closer you grow to Christ, the less attractive the things of the world will appear. Let your prayer be, "Dear Jesus, help me to fall in love with you more and more every single day of my life. Teach me how to truly live in your presence 24/7."

"When I was little, I said 'Sorry' to my mom and she said, 'You should be.' After that I never wanted to say sorry to my mom again. It ate me up inside, until two years ago when we talked about it and resolved the issue."

—Alison, 17

Ladies, when you're praying this way, you're also being a godly role model to your daughter. When you turn down her request to watch a specific movie, she knows that you're not going to go see it later with your husband.

When you monitor what she reads and the time she spends on the computer, she knows that you're not reading trashy romance novels while she's at school or entering chat rooms and flirting with men. In other words, she knows beyond doubt that you live what you say. Your words match your actions.

Your daughter desperately needs to see you as her godly role model. She needs to see that the blouses you wear aren't too low, too tight, or too revealing. She needs to see that your jeans aren't

Here for You   147

pasted on and that you don't look longingly at a handsome man walking by. She needs to see a lifestyle of integrity through your actions, your words, and your character.

When you're accidentally given too much change at the grocery store, she needs to see you give it back. When you're stopped for exceeding the speed limit, she needs to notice that you accept responsibility instead of making excuses or being defensive. She needs to hear you ask forgiveness. She needs to see your devoted love for God.

Will you make a holy covenant with your daughter to be her godly role model?

#2: "I make a sacred covenant with you to be here for you; to be your safety net."

I (Susie) was talking with Ed, the youth pastor at our church, and my heart broke as he told me about Aimee.

> Aimee was with the wrong group of friends, and she knew it. She disobeyed her parents and went to a party she didn't have permission to attend. Things got out of hand, and a guy—whom Aimee didn't know—started putting the moves on her.
>
> At first she was flattered by all the attention he was giving her, and when he suggested they leave the party, she willingly went. He stopped at a convenience store and bought a six-pack of beer and came back to his truck and started drinking. He offered Aimee a can, but she turned him down. "Just take me home," she said.
>
> By this time she knew she was in over her head and just wanted to get away from this guy. When he told her he was going to take her to his apartment, she refused. "There's no way my mom will let me stay out any later," she said.
>
> So this guy told her to call her mom and lie to her. "Tell her you're spending the night with a friend," he said. Then he

thrust his cell phone into Aimee's hand and watched as she dialed home.

Her mom answered the phone, and Aimee purposely asked to spend the night with a friend her mom never let her hang out with. Unfortunately, her mom said okay this time.

Aimee's heart began to race. She hung up, turned to the guy, and said, "My mom won't let me."

"Nope," he said. "You're lying. I heard her. She said you could!"

Aimee didn't have the social skills or boundaries set that she should have, and she was scared to death. She felt she had no choice but to go with the guy. He was already angry, and she was frightened he'd become more furious the more he drank.

He took her to his apartment and raped her.

It took Aimee four hours to tell me what happened. As she did, I wept inside for her. Why didn't her mom say no like she usually did? Why had Aimee disobeyed in the first place?

It was clear that Aimee needed a safety net. I talked it over with my wife, and we've now created a safety net for our nine-year-old daughter. We're also going to use this safety net for the entire youth group.

We sat down with our daughter and said, "Honey, in a few years you'll be going out with your friends and staying up later than you're allowed to now. There may come a time when you're in danger and need us in a hurry. So let's use our dog's name—Midnight—and if you ever phone us and simply say 'Midnight,' we'll know you need our help immediately. We won't question you. We'll simply come get you and bring you home."

"I love it when my mom talks with me about God."

—Phoebe, 14

I then told the entire youth group that they too had a code word: Midnight. "Anytime you're somewhere you shouldn't be, anytime things get out of hand, anytime you need immediate assistance, all you have to do is call us and say 'Midnight.' We'll come get you immediately."

We're so glad Ed and his wife, Lori, are willing and available to be a safety net for the students in their youth group. But wouldn't it be even more amazing if every girl had a safety net in her *mother*?!

Moms, as you covenant to be a safety net to your daughter, you're telling her that you'll be there for her. Decide together what her code word will be, and let her know that if ever she calls and utters that word, you'll react with immediacy and come get her. Know that this isn't the time to ask questions, nor is it the time for a lecture.

There will be a time to discuss disobedience, friend choices, and decisions/consequences later. But for the time at hand, promise to be her safety net. She needs to know that she can call you anytime, from anyplace, for any reason and be assured of your rescue. Knowing that will give her a security beyond description.

"I love it when my mom is understanding and patient."
—Samantha, 17

Moms, will you be there for your daughter? Will you pledge to be her safety net?

#3: *"I make a sacred covenant with you to pray for you every day."*

When your daughter realizes that you actually walk into the throne room of heaven and petition the King of Kings for her well-being and for His favor, she'll begin to exhibit a healthy confidence that no one can shake.

I (Susie) am fortunate to have a huge spiritual heritage. My grandparents, parents, aunts, and uncles all pray(ed) for me daily. I know that because they told me. They wanted me to know that they were talking to God about *me*! That not only gave me confidence, but it made me want to live up to that incredible spiritual heritage.

Because of the great amount of time my relatives spent in prayer for God's hand to be on my life, I didn't even *want* to rebel. I wanted their prayers to be worth their efforts.

"I love it when my mom dances with me."

—Heather, 16

Several times growing up, I "caught" my mom praying and reading her Bible. Do you realize what that does for a child? It made me realize how important her relationship with Christ was! I learned, too, that my own relationship with Christ needed to take on the role of importance God desired for me to give Him.

I remember one particular night when I was home from college on Christmas break. I had the flu and was up at all hours. My most recent trip to the bathroom happened to be around five-thirty or six in the morning.

As I walked down the hall, I noticed a light on in the den. When I went to turn it off, I saw my dad kneeling by the couch with his Bible. "Dad, what are you doing up so early?" I asked.

"Oh, I'm praying for you. This is where I pray for you every morning," he said. I went back to bed ever so grateful for godly parents who *daily* entered the throne room of God on my behalf.

Moms, will you make a sacred oath to pray for your daughter every single day? I can't think of a more important way to spend your time than talking to the Creator of the universe about your daughter—praying for His hand of blessing on her life, asking for His Spirit to deepen her faith, praying for her choices regarding friends and relationships, praying for her future husband and her family, asking God to keep her pure, pleading with Him to watch over her and teach her that she is dearly loved and valued.

#4: "I make a sacred covenant to consistently pray with you."

I recently spoke at a women's retreat, and afterward a mom approached me about her daughter. "She's impossible to communicate with, and I just don't know what to do!" she said in desperation.

"Do you pray for your daughter?" I asked.

"Oh yes. I pray for her all the time."

"That's great," I said. "Do you pray *with* her?"

The woman was silent and shocked. When she finally spoke, she said, "Oh my! That would really be uncomfortable!"

Yes, moms, it may be uncomfortable to pray with your daughters—especially if you're not in the habit of doing so—but it's an essential ingredient in your covenant and in her spiritual well-being.

"My mom and I argue a lot, but we never go to bed without talking about it."

—Christina, 18

Not only did I know that my parents prayed *for* me, but also they demonstrated the importance of prayer by praying *with* me. I can remember times when Dad would get up and turn off the TV and say, "Let's gather for prayer."

We'd actually kneel as a family. My brother, Kent, would kneel in front of the couch. I'd kneel by the piano bench. Mom would kneel by the sofa. And Dad would kneel in front of his recliner. One by one, we'd lift our concerns to the Lord.

We didn't do this every night. My parents wanted us to learn how to pray independently as well as together. But we did it often, and Kent and I were never doubtful of the power of prayer. We grew up knowing there was nothing too small and nothing too big to pray about. We realized if it concerned us, it concerned our heavenly Father.

This also taught us to be comfortable with praying in front of others. Yes, prayer was a private matter, but it was also a group matter. We learned to share our concerns with each other and then to take them directly to the Lord. In doing so, we also learned to watch and wait for His answers.

Moms, do you realize that every time you drive your daughter somewhere, you have a captive audience? It's you and her in a locked car! Take advantage of it! Instead of turning on the tunes, take turns uttering a sentence prayer back and forth. Teach your daughter that you can literally pray about anything and everything. Here's an example:

Mom: Father, please help Heather to remember what she's studied today during her history final.

Heather: Dear Jesus, thanks that we're having hamburgers today in the school cafeteria.

Mom: Father, thank you giving us a great night's sleep. I sure needed it!

Heather: Jesus, I need your boldness today in biology class when they start talking about evolution.

Mom: Thanks, Father, that we get to have pizza together as a family tonight.

> "My mom got a new job that was really stressful, and I felt she was taking her stress out on me. I asked if we could start praying together. It's amazing how much that has helped!"
>
> —Mindee, 15

Heather: Lord, please help Dad get that promotion he's been wanting.

By teaching your daughter to pray sentence prayers out loud—and in a back-and-forth manner with you—you're helping her become comfortable telling God whatever is on her heart. She'll begin to realize that it's not just the huge things she needs to take to God, but that He delights in simply hearing her chat with Him. He loves to hear His children talk with Him about everything!

It may not be possible for you to pray every day *with* your daughter because of your work schedule or because she may be away at college or for a variety of other reasons. But when it *is* possible, sit on the edge of her bed with the lights out and lift your hearts in prayer together. And vary the way you pray. Sometimes kneel with your daughter. No, this doesn't ensure our prayers get through any faster, but it sure reminds us quickly of our humility and God's greatness.

Moms, will you promise to pray with your daughter consistently? Again, it may not be possible to pray *with* her every day. But will you do it often—when you can? As you do, the bond between the two of you will strengthen. Know why? Because you're weaving a tightly knit band of three cords—between you, your daughter, and God. That's a sacred bond!

"I love it when my mom organizes everything herself so our family is well taken care of."

—Savannah, 18

#5: *"I make a sacred covenant to help you unfold the unique personality and gifts with which you've been blessed."*

My mother was a detailed person.

Very organized.

Everything had a place, and everything was usually in its place.

154 SHELLENBERGER • GOWLER

I'm just the opposite. I lose my keys, my purse, and my passport at least once a week.

My mom was a planner. I'm spontaneous.

Mom saved. I spend.

Mom enjoyed cooking. I love to be outdoors.

She thought before she spoke. I speak . . . and then wonder if I should have.

She was disciplined. I'm not.

She'd work ahead of time on things that were due; she'd do a little each day until the task was completed. I wait till the last minute and pull an all-nighter.

> "I love it when my mom sings worship songs while she's doing the dishes."
>
> —Meagan, 18

When she began to realize our differences, she didn't try to fit me into her personality mold. She gave me room to be myself. She encouraged me in sports, even though she never participated. She enjoyed hearing about my water-skiing trips with the youth group, though she was afraid of water.

She helped me join a craft club when I said I was bored and wanted to make something.

She didn't force me to cook or stay indoors. She helped me unpack the creativity that God had blessed me with. She took me to the library and introduced me to biographies of creative people. She encouraged me to write and sing and act.

And she allowed me to sit in my room for hours on end with the door closed so I could write. And write. And write. She didn't understand it, but she gave me the space and freedom to do it.

And my dad—though saturated in the business world—consistently told me over and over that I could do anything I wanted if I was willing to work hard enough. "Why don't you create some greeting cards?" he'd suggest.

Or "I'll bet you could write a song if you wanted to."

Or "If I make a high-jump set, would you be willing to work until you can clear three feet? I'll pay you a dollar when you can jump three feet!"

To a soon-to-be fourth-grader during summer vacation, that was the highlight of my days and kept me from getting bored. It also taught me that if I stuck with something long enough, I could accomplish it.

I still have the plaque he made me, complete with a framed dollar bill, expressing how proud he was that I had met my goal five months later.

My parents gave me the freedom to develop the gifts and abilities God

"I love it when my mom doesn't interrupt me, but it doesn't happen very often."

—Elizabeth, 16

placed within me. Of course, I needed guidance, and they stepped in to guide me even though their interests and skills were often in other areas.

Perhaps you love to run. It energizes you and frees your mind. If your daughter truly isn't interested in joining you, don't force her. Find out what she *is* interested in. This can often be a process. Often a child or teen doesn't know what her gifts are, and she has to try several different things to discover her interests and her abilities.

Be patient. Be willing to endure the drums, ballet, sewing classes, swim meets, spelling bees—whatever it takes to help her discover the gifts and personality God has placed within her.

Why is this so important? Because God has created her to be an individual, not a carbon copy of you. Instead of yearning for her to be more like you, celebrate the differences you share. Learn to respect and admire the funny twist she spins on a story or the attention to detail she puts into painting the mural on her bedroom wall.

As you help her unfold her unique personality, you're helping her come into herself, believe in herself, and learn how to use her gifts to glorify the Giver. Moms, will you covenant with your daughter to help her unfold the unique personality and gifts with which she's been blessed?

First Things First

Before you make this five-part sacred oath with your daughter, first make it with God. Tell Him how desperately you want to live out all five pieces of this covenant. Acknowledge that you can't do it on your own, and you need His supernatural help.

Now take a few minutes to pray through each part of this covenant. Commit all five areas to God, realizing that by making this sacred oath, you're establishing a covenant with your heavenly Father that will *not* be broken.

After you've prayed through each step of the covenant, plan a special time with your daughter. Take her out for dinner, make her favorite dish at home, go hiking with her, or spend the night in a hotel—something special—and explain that you love her unequivocally.

Tell her that you've made a sacred oath on her behalf to God, and now you want to make it to her. If she has questions about an oath, read chapters 4 and 5 of this book together again.

After you've given the entire covenant to your daughter, seal it by placing a special piece of covenant jewelry around her neck. (Of course, you don't *have* to use our Closer jewelry—anything special will work. But the Closer jewelry has part of the covenant engraved on it.) To order the jewelry we've had custom designed for this experience, go to *www.closermomsanddaughters.com.*

After you've clasped the necklace around your daughter's neck, cement the covenant in prayer together.

Stuff I Wish My Daughter Would Tell Me

- *she loves me*
- *what happened at school today*
- *what she and her friends talk about*
- *that sometimes she's wrong*
- *what she's afraid of*
- *what God is teaching her*
- *she appreciates it when I make her favorite meal*
- *the questions she has about sex*
- *she trusts me*
- *why she's sad*
- *she's proud to introduce me to her friends*
- *about the guys she has crushes on*
- *the little everyday things—what she had for lunch, what made her laugh today, how she did on her science test*

CHAPTER 11

Making a Covenant: For Daughters Only

[A] mother is one to whom you hurry when you are troubled.
—Emily Dickinson

We've talked about a lot of different things in this book, haven't we? But the underlying purpose is to make a covenant with God and to make a covenant with your mom. In previous chapters, you've had opportunities to make a covenant with God. Now it's time to talk about covenant-making with your mom.

Girls, there are five parts to the covenant you're being challenged to make with your mom. The only way you can be successful at making and keeping this sacred oath with her is by first having a covenant with your heavenly Father.

Even though you've had opportunities to do so already, let's be sure you feel grounded spiritually, okay?

1. I've experienced and expressed remorse for my sins. I've repented in sorrow to Christ and have sought His forgiveness. _____ True _____ False
2. I believe Christ has forgiven my sins. (See Romans 3:22–24.) _____ True _____ False
3. I have placed my faith in Christ and have given Him control of my life. _____ True _____ False
4. I still mess up, but when I do, I ask God to forgive me, and He does. _____ True _____ False
5. I understand that prayer and reading my Bible are necessary ingredients for my spiritual growth. _____ True _____ False

6. I have made a covenant to serve God the rest of my life.

_____ True _____ False

Girls, if you couldn't answer true to any of the above statements, will you take the time to make it right before God *now*? If you don't have a genuine covenant with God, you can't have a genuine covenant with your mom. Is there any spiritual business you need to do with the Lord? Do it now!

Daughter's Five-Part Covenant to Mom

Daughter: "*I make a sacred covenant with you . . .*
#1: to love you NMW—No Matter What."
#2: to pray for you every day."
#3: to consistently pray with you."
#4: to be honest with you."
#5: to respect the position of authority God has placed you in over my life."

"*I love when my mom spends quality time with me. That can be anything from going to coffee to spending time talking and listening, or anything that's just together.*"
—Whitney, 22

Let's discuss each facet of this sacred covenant, so you'll have a full understanding of what you're promising your mom.

#1: "I make a sacred covenant with you to love you NMW—no matter what."

Girls, it's easy for moms to assume you love them because of what they *do* for you. *As long as I provide her with an allowance and let her have friends over, she loves me,* your mom may think.

But what would happen if your mom became ill and lost her job? Your allowance may suddenly become nonexistent. Because of an illness, she may not be able to handle company in the home. Would your feelings or your commitment to her change?

I hope not.

Your mom is human.

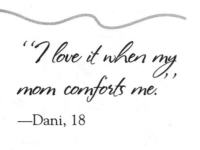

"*I love it when my mom comforts me.*"

—Dani, 18

What?! My mom is . . . human?

And because she's human, she'll blow it from time to time. When your mom makes a mistake, it's God's will that you continue to love her.

Ever have trouble coming up with the perfect gift for your mom's birthday or for Christmas? The best gift you can ever give her is the assurance and the promise that you'll love her forever NMW—no matter what.

When she's old and can't walk without help . . .

When she battles menopause and cries unexpectedly . . .

When she longs to buy you a new dress for the prom but can't afford to . . .

When she mistakenly blames you instead of your brother . . .

When she's eighty-five and struggling with Alzheimer's and fails to remember your name . . .

NMW, your mom needs your love.

Girls, when you commit to loving your mom no matter what, an indescribable bond begins to develop between the two of you that's almost impossible to break.

Does that mean I'll never get upset with her?

No. You're still human. And there will always be things you disagree on, different viewpoints. But committing to love someone NMW surpasses emotion.

It's a decision.

A pledge.

And when you commit to loving your mom NMW, you'll also

be learning how to commit to love someone else very important in your life—your future husband.

Girls, will you make a sacred oath to love your mom through the good, the bad, the confusing, the disagreements, the "she shouldn't haves," NMW? If you will, it'll change your relationship forever!

#2: "I make a sacred covenant with you to pray for you every day."

I (Susie) met sixteen-year-old Lauren on a two-week missions trip to Bolivia. She was assigned to two roommates in her hotel room. Imagine my surprise when one of her roommates pulled me aside and said, "Susie, I woke up at five-thirty this morning because I heard something really soft. I couldn't figure out what it was. I listened and listened and finally got out of bed. The soft sounds seemed to be coming from the closet. So I opened the door, and there was Lauren! She was in the closet praying! Cool, huh?"

"I love it when my mom buys me ice cream, reads to me, makes me breakfast."

—Beth, 19

I approached Lauren and told her I thought it was awesome that she was praying so early in the morning. "Oh, it's no big deal," she said. "It's something I do every morning. I didn't want to wake my roommates, so I thought sitting in the closet would muffle my sounds, but I guess I got carried away."

"Lauren, what do you talk to God about each morning? Anything and everything?"

"Yeah, pretty much. But I also make a point to pray for my mom. We've promised to pray for each other every day. And you know? Ever since we started praying for each other so much, we get along a lot better!"

Gweneth's mom recently left the family. "It broke my heart," Gweneth says. "I don't understand it. She started withdrawing, and she just didn't seem like herself. Then last month she announced that she had never loved my dad and had to find herself, and she left us. I still cry every day. I miss her like crazy. I don't agree with what she's done, but I still love her. She's my mom! I'll always love her—even when she does something that hurts us or doesn't make sense. I'm going to keep praying for her every day."

Girls, it's impossible to stay angry at someone you pray for every day. The more you pray for your mom, the more you'll fall in love with her. You'll begin to see her through the eyes of her Creator, and that will help you understand her better.

I pray for my entire family, individually, every single day. I count it as a privilege that I can actually talk to the Creator of the universe about each one of them and ask for Him to help them make wise choices, to know they're loved, and to be kept safe. I'll never know until I get to heaven the difference my prayers make. But even though I can't always see the difference now, I know prayer *is* making a difference in their lives every single day.

Girls, will you make an oath to pray for your mom every single day? And then let her know! She'll revel with joy in the commitment you've made to talk with God about her personal concerns!

> "My mom and I used to fight a lot. After talking heart-to-heart one night, I realized how mean I had been to her. We prayed together and asked for forgiveness: me for saying hurtful things, and my mom for taking her anger and stress out on me."
>
> —Libby, 18

#3: "I make a sacred covenant to consistently pray with you."

It's not enough to simply pray *for* your mom; it's also important to pray *with* her as often as you can. Did you know that God has a special promise for those who pray *together*? Check out Matthew 18:20: "For where two or three come together in my name, there am I with them."

There is power in prayer! And there's power when you pray *with* someone. God honors that effort.

But I've never prayed with my mom before, you may be thinking. That's okay. It may be a little uncomfortable at first, but I don't know any Christian mom who wouldn't be honored for her daughter to approach her and ask to pray together. What a gift!

"I love it when my mom cries with me."

—Sadie, 15

It may not be possible for you to pray every day *with* your mom because of her work schedule, because you may be away at college, or because of a variety of reasons. But when it *is* possible, make it a point to pray together. And vary the way you pray. Sometimes ask your mom to kneel with you. Other times sit across from each other. Sometimes pray back-and-forth sentence prayers. Other times simply lift your concerns to the Father.

If you think your mom may be resistant to doing this, try a different approach. Say something like, "Mom, every Thursday night at ten, I'm going to be kneeling here at the couch. When you see me, just know that I'm praying for us. If you'd like to join me, that would be great! But if not, that's okay. I just want you to know why I'm here every Thursday and what I'll be doing."

I guarantee after a month of praying, you'll notice a difference in your relationship with your mom!

Girls, will you promise to pray with your mom consistently? Again, it may not be possible to pray *with* her every day. But will you do it often—when you can? As you do, the bond between the two of you will strengthen. Know why? Because you're weaving a tightly knit band of three cords—between you, your mom, and God. *That's* a sacred bond!

#4: "I make a sacred covenant to be honest with you."

Deidre's curfew is midnight on the weekends. She and her friends made a few wrong turns last night, and she didn't get home until 1:30 a.m.

The next morning at breakfast her mom says, "Deidre, were you home by curfew?"

Deidre says, "Are you kidding, Mom? I know when curfew is! I wouldn't think of missing it."

Has Deidre been honest with her mom?

She really hasn't, has she?

She averted the truth and alluded to something else. She deliberately deceived her mom into believing curfew was made.

> *"I love it when my mom comes into my room and talks with me before bed."*
>
> —Sophia, 15

Maybe you consider something along that line a little white lie. And perhaps you believe little white lies aren't real lies. But the truth is, a lie is simply being deceptive. God hates lying so much, He included it in the Ten Commandments.

Your mom deserves your honesty—even when it means you'll suffer the consequences, and even when it's difficult. Girls, by becoming honest *now*, you're developing a lifestyle of integrity that will set you above the crowd for years down the road.

By being honest, you're developing a trustworthy character—someone your future husband will delight in, one whom your future boss and co-workers will appreciate, and one your children will someday come to admire.

Jesus was honest, and He expects the same of you. Will you pledge a lifetime of honesty with your mom? By developing this honesty with her, you're also establishing a secure respect and admiration between the two of you. And *that's* something that will last a lifetime!

#5: *"I make a sacred covenant to respect the position of authority God has placed you in over my life."*

Let's take a peek at Ephesians 6:1–3: "Children, obey your parents in the Lord, for this is right. 'Honor your father and mother'—which is the first commandment with a promise—'that it may go well with you and that you may enjoy long life on the earth.'"

Did you realize there's a promise in store for you when you honor and obey your parents? It's the promise of a long and full life. What a blessing!

"I love it when my mom plays the piano for me at night to help me sleep."

—Suni, 16

"My mom and I disagree on lots of things," Chelsey says. "But I respect her authority."

"I've learned I can say anything to my mom as long as I do it kindly and with respect," Brooke says.

Honoring and obeying your parents doesn't mean you have to agree with them. Because of the difference in your personalities and the difference in your ages, you'll probably often disagree. That's okay. You can disagree and still honor and obey your parents.

This is how it works: God is in authority over your parents. And He's placed them in authority over you. So you prove your love for God by loving and honoring your parents.

Do you know what it does for a parent when her child honors and respects her? It makes her proud! "Staci has her own opinions about things," fifty-two-year-old Monica says. "And I'm proud of her for thinking independently. The thing that makes me most proud as a mom, though, is the fact that she honors what I say. She doesn't always agree, but she honors and respects the fact that my word is the final word."

Is there ever a time when I shouldn't obey my parents?

Good question.

God never contradicts himself. He tells you to honor your parents *in the Lord.* (Reread Ephesians 6:1–3.) In other words, he's talking about Christian parents. Christian parents won't tell you to do something that is disobedient to God.

For example, if your mom says, "Honey, I'm craving beef stroganoff and there's only one restaurant in town that makes it. Unfortunately, we're out of grocery money, so I want you to dress up as a pumpkin and head to Mercer's Italian Restaurant. When they see a pumpkin walk through the door, they'll be distracted and won't notice when I scoop all the stroganoff from the kitchen into this big bag. Just keep talking and saying pumpkin-like things, and I'll be able to steal all the stroganoff we can eat.

"After I've filled the bag and left, pour some baby oil on the floor on your way out. That's in case they come to their senses and start to chase us—they'll slip on the oil and you'll be able to escape safely. Let's go!"

Of course, in that situation, you'd need to disobey your mom because she's asking you to break the law by stealing, and she's also asking you to disobey God.

"My mom struggles with depression. It got so bad she wouldn't go to church. At one point I used guilt to make her go. Finally we sat down and talked about her depression. I understand a little better now."

—Roxane, 16

(I realize that's a crazy example, but you asked, so I had to come up with something.)

Seriously, the more you honor and respect your parents, the more they'll trust you. Want more responsibility? Honor your mom. Want more freedom? Respect and obey your mom.

Want your mom to see you as mature and dependable? Obey her even when you don't agree with her. Girls, will you promise to obey your mom's authority? Remember, she hasn't demanded this role on her own; God has given it to her. By honoring her

"I love it when my mom holds me. It makes me feel secure."
—Gabi, 14

authority, you're demonstrating your love for God. And *that's* something He rewards!

First Things First

Before you make this five-part sacred oath with your mom, first make it with God. Tell Him how desperately you want to live out all five pieces of this covenant. Acknowledge that you can't do it on your own, and you need His supernatural help.

Now take a few minutes to pray through each part of this covenant. Commit all five areas to God, realizing that by making this sacred oath, you're establishing a covenant with your heavenly Father that will *not* be broken.

After you've prayed through each step of the covenant, ask your mom if the two of you can have a special time together. Suggest going out to dinner or serving your mom her favorite meal at home. Or offer to go to the symphony with her, see a play, rent a video, or even spend the night in a hotel—and as you do so, explain that you love her unequivocally.

Tell her that you've made a sacred oath on her behalf to God, and now you want to make it to her. If she has questions about an oath, read chapters 4 and 5 of this book together again.

After you've given the entire covenant to your mom, seal it by placing a special piece of covenant jewelry around her neck. (To order the jewelry we've had custom designed for this experience, go to *www.closermomsand daughters.com*.)

After you've clasped the necklace around your mom's neck, cement the covenant in prayer together.

"I love it when my mom does crazy stuff with me."
—Lily, 12

CHAPTER 12

Keeping the Covenant:
Practical Ideas for Moms

*Of all the haunting moments of motherhood, few rank with hearing
your own words come out of your daughter's mouth.*
—Victoria Secunda

Now that you've made this sacred oath with God and with your
daughter, how in the world will you maintain it? Think of a camp-
fire. To maintain the flame, you have to keep the fire stoked. Your
covenant can be thought of in the same way. It won't maintain
itself. Just like a fire, you'll need to continue to prod the flame to
keep it burning brightly. Your head may already be spinning with
ideas, but allow us to give a few suggestions.

Four Fabulous Flame Keepers

*#1: Just Between Us: Mom-Daughter
Journaling*

We've tried out this idea with
moms and daughters and have seen it
work so well, we've decided to designate an entire appendix for this (see
page 196. It consists of passing a notebook between the two of you with
questions and comments from each one
to the other. We'll go into more detail
beginning on page 202.

*"I love it when my
mom writes me love
notes and leaves
them in my room."*
—Staci, 18

#2: Just Between Us: Date Your Daughter

In an earlier chapter I (Susie) shared the memory I have of my mom taking me to dinner every Monday evening during my high school years. It was never extravagant—it was always a dinner purchased with a buy-one-get-one-free coupon. But it wasn't the actual meal that I remember; it was simply being with my mom, just the two of us.

Your schedule (or your daughter's schedule) may not allow for a weekly date. It may take a few times to discover what works best for the two of you, but when you find your routine, make it consistent. If you decide on two Saturday morning breakfasts a month, stick with it! Strive to make this time with your daughter so special that nothing else seems as important as keeping your commitment to be together.

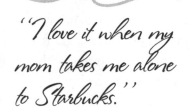

"I love it when my mom takes me alone to Starbucks."

—Jasmine, 16

Of course, there are always exceptions. Don't feel guilty when you *do* have to cancel or postpone; just don't do it often. Here are some ideas for mom/daughter dates:

• breakfast, brunch, lunch, dinner, late-night snacks, or coffee
• doing a Bible study together
• craft-making sessions in a spare room, the basement, or your kitchen (candle-making, learning to wallpaper or stencil, sewing a new wardrobe, making greeting cards together, etc.)
• baking a variety of simple and extravagant desserts together
• reading a book together and discussing each chapter
• shopping at a thrift store
• giving each other a pedicure or manicure
• shopping for something new for her bedroom or bathroom . . . just because

- seeing a chick flick together and grabbing ice cream afterward so you can discuss the movie
- making and delivering a meal to a sick friend or loved one . . . or even to the couple from church with the new baby

But before you actually do any of the above, ask your daughter what she'd like to do and take both of your schedules and time frames into consideration when making plans.

"I love it when my mom gives me good advice but doesn't pry too much when giving it."
—Lorissa, 17

#3: *Just Between Us: Mom/Daughter Retreat*

Just like camp—only for a weekend—this special time together should be filled with your and your daughter's favorite activities. If T-shirts or sweatshirts are your thing, get a special shirt for the weekend that you'll always remember represents your very own retreat.

This can be as simple or extravagant as your budget and schedule allow. But whether you're going on a cruise or staying in a hotel, get away. It doesn't have to be far enough to fly, but make it a *trip*. After all, *getting there* can be half the fun!

Does your daughter love horses? Make plans to take her horseback riding. Or jet-skiing. Snorkeling. Rafting trip down a lazy river. Snow-skiing. Camping in a tent. Get tickets to the ballet or opera. See a well-known play. How about taking a trip to the nation's largest mall—the Mall of America in Minneapolis? Use your creativity. The sky's the limit!

#4: *Just Between Us: Communicate!*

This is the most important way to maintain the covenant with your daughter. It sounds elementary, but it's often more difficult than it sounds. It's also absolutely essential! Communicating includes prayer for and with your daughter, written expressions of love and affirmation, verbal affirmation, and physical touch.

Leave notes for your daughter on her bathroom mirror, inside her car, tucked in her coat pocket, inside her purse. Echo your love for her through greeting cards, letters, sticky notes, etc.

Talk, talk, talk! At the same time, be aware of the times she needs her own space and privacy. And realize that the times she's most willing to talk may not be the easiest for you. Her favorite time to chat may be at 11:30 p.m. Or if she's a morning person, it may be at 6:00 a.m. Be willing to flex your comfort zone and meet her where and when she's ready to communicate.

"I love it when my mom takes time to play a game with me."

—Annette, 17

And even though you may be a great communicator, know there will be times of distance—simply because you're both human. My friend Jennifer has a close relationship with her fourteen-year-old daughter, Stephanie, but recently they experienced a distant spell.

"We went through an entire week," Jennifer says, "where there was just a weird distance between us. I didn't know if Stephanie felt it or not. I just assumed it was normal fourteen-year-old stuff. But toward the end of the week, I couldn't stand it any longer and finally brought it up.

"I didn't put her on the defensive. I just asked, 'Stephanie, do you feel there's a distance between us?' And she immediately started crying and said she felt it too."

"Well, you both probably were just so into your own schedules, you kind of drifted apart for a while, right?" I asked.

"No, I think it was actually more than that," Jennifer responded.

"What was it?" I prodded.

"Well, we spent almost all of Labor Day weekend shopping, and I think I just got on her nerves. In fact, I know I did. I can even pinpoint it.

"We were at Bath and Body Works in the mall, and I was looking for a specific scent. I rushed from display to display like a madwoman. I was squirting various sprays and almost bumping into people I was in such a hurry. I was being really intense about finding this scent.

"Stephanie finally said, 'Mom! Would you just stop? Slow down!'

"And I said, 'If I'm embarrassing you, just go on into the mall.'

"She didn't. She stayed with me. But I realized at that moment I was kind of being a menace to the other shoppers as well as an embarrassment to my daughter.

"At the end of the week when I mentioned the distance between us, we were able to talk it out and move on."

"I love it when my mom doesn't force me to tell her things."
—Evette, 13

Moms, be aware of your intensity, and know that small things from your perspective can be seen as large things from your daughter's perspective. You don't want to embarrass your daughter. Just be yourself; you'll make her proud. Determine to communicate; pace yourself during the process!

By practicing specific disciplines that are created just for you and your daughter, you'll not only be maintaining your sacred covenant with her; you'll also be making it stronger.

Chapter 13

Keeping the Covenant: Practical Ideas for Daughters

All that I am, or hope to be, I owe to my angel mother.
—Abraham Lincoln

Now that you've made this sacred oath with God and with your mom, how in the world will you maintain it? Think of a swimming pool. It can be used to strengthen your muscles if you consistently swim. It can be used for relaxation purposes—imagine jumping into the clear, cool water at the end of a hot, humid day! And it can also be used for entertainment with a group of friends and your favorite tunes nearby.

"I love it when my mom lies in bed with me and just talks girl talk."
—Jessica, 21

But to get the most out of your swimming pool, there are certain things you have to do to keep it at its best. You need to clean it, check the chlorine levels, and keep water in it.

Think of your covenant in the same way. It won't maintain itself. Just like with a swimming pool, you'll need to provide continued maintenance to keep it at its best. Your head may already be spinning with ideas, but let's use the swimming pool analogy to get you started.

Pool (and Covenant) Maintenance

#1: Clean It

To keep your pool in pristine order, you'll need to remove the leaves, insects, and clutter that accumulate. Outdoor swimming pools aren't the only things that gather clutter; relationships do as well. It's a given: Your relationship with Mom will become cluttered from time to time. By "cleaning" it on a regular basis, though, you'll still be able to live out your sacred oath.

Think for a moment about the clutter that tends to come between you and your mom. Grab your pen and list the clutter that can hinder your relationship with one another. Next to the clutter, explain how it hurts your relationship. I'll get you started, and you finish the list, okay?

> *"I love it when my mom reads the Bible to me at night."*
> —Chrissie, 16

- Sarcasm: When I use it on my mom, she feels I'm being disrespectful. When she uses it on me, I feel degraded.
- _____
- _____
- _____
- _____

You know how to clean the clutter from a swimming pool, but how do you specifically remove the clutter from a relationship? **Communication!** Tell your mom (as soon as you've finished this chapter) that you don't want to be sarcastic with her.

Give her permission to gently call it to your attention whenever you deliver a sarcastic response. But also ask if you can have the same privilege. In other words, if your mom is sarcastic to you, ask her ahead of time if it's okay for you to let her know right at that moment that your feelings were hurt by her response. And, of course, this needs to be done in a gentle way, not from the top of your lungs.

"I'm naturally a sarcastic person," seventeen-year-old Marissa says. "It's like . . . you know . . . part of my personality. So when my mom told me my sarcasm was hurting her, it was as though she was saying, 'Change your personality.' It really made me mad.

"So she asked me to just pray about it. It took a couple of months, but I finally began to realize that sarcasm really *can* hurt. Yeah, it's funny sometimes, but I don't want to hurt someone just to get a laugh. I'm still sarcastic, but not nearly as much. I'm working on it. God has really helped me. And the cool thing? He's showing me other ways I can be funny without slamming someone."

"I love it when my mom points out the good in me instead of focusing on the bad."
—Heidi, 17

As you openly discuss things together—in a calm and mature way—you'll be consistently removing the clutter from your relationship.

#2: *Check the Chlorine Levels*

Maybe you've watched the pool guy at the YMCA or the local gym check the chlorine levels in the pool. He has a special instrument that he places in the water, and he gets on his knees, placing himself as close to the water as possible to get the best reading.

There were a couple of key phrases in that sentence. Did you catch them? *On his knees* and as *close to the water as possible*.

Remember, your sacred covenant is threefold. It's between you, God, and your mom. Christ wants you as close to Him as you can possibly get. He also wants you as close to your mom as you can possibly get. The way you draw closer to Christ is by being on your knees—or through prayer. (Reading the Bible also keeps you close to Him.)

As you develop a strong, powerful prayer line that shoots directly into the kingdom of heaven, don't simply pray for yourself; pray for your mom as well. (After all, praying for her daily is part of your covenant with her.) Lift her needs to the Father. Ask for His protection over her. Plead for His hand of favor to cover her. And ask Him to greatly bless your relationship with her. Do you have any idea how much it will mean to your mom to know that you're on your knees for her? Wow! It'll be life-changing.

Do you have to be on your knees?

No.

But falling on our knees before our heavenly Father creates a genuine humility in us. And as you pray, lift to the Lord the concerns you have regarding your relationship with Mom. The things that bug you, how you respond to her, everything that's part of your relationship needs to be brought before the Father.

"I love it when my mom tells her friends how special I am to her."

—Marian, 16

As you pray consistently for your mom, you'll automatically be drawing closer to God *and* to her. The pool guy gets as close to the water as he can before he places the measuring instrument into the pool. Make an effort not only to be emotionally and spiritually close to your mom but to get close to her physically as well.

Why is this important?

Just as it helps the pool guy ensure all the levels are where they're supposed to be, it will help you and your mom make sure your emotional and verbal levels are healthy. It's amazing how physical closeness can reveal that, but it can!

"I love it when my mom gives me godly advice."
—Breanna, 16

"I'm a natural touchy-feely-friendly person," Corina says. "I don't know where I got that from, because my mom's never been a big hugger. I *want* to hug her, but it feels weird, you know?

"It was hard, but I finally just asked her, 'Mom, how come you seem so uncomfortable when I try to hug you?' And she explained that she'd been abused when she was a teen. Wow. Talk about shock! Well, that put everything in perspective right away.

"I know it was tough for her to tell me that, but I'm so glad she did. She told me that most of the time when I approached her for a hug, I'd come up from behind, and it always caught her off guard. She explained it would be much more comfortable to her if I'd approach her from the side or the front.

"Who would have known? Sheesh! I'm so glad I said something. That makes total sense to me. So we're getting better at the hugs now; I just make an effort to not sneak up on her."

Make an effort to touch your mom; hug her often, rub her shoulders, pat her on the back. The more you do this, the closer you'll both feel to each other. This may be uncomfortable at first if you're not a naturally touchy person.

Don't go overboard. I'm not suggesting you constantly be touching your mom. But make an effort to give her a hug or touch her in some way every single day.

#3: *Enjoy It!*

Okay, you've taken the time to clean your pool and get rid of the clutter, and you're carefully watching the chlorine levels by maintaining a consistent prayer life that includes talking to God on behalf of your mom. You understand she needs support too. What's next?

Now it's time to *enjoy* your pool, uh . . . I mean your mom!

Think back to when you were younger. Remember a time when you received a really cool game or toy for Christmas. It captured your attention for an hour or so, and then you were simply bored with it.

Maybe you didn't take the time to read all the instructions and learn about *all* the different things your toy could do. You were so excited to have it, you simply did the obvious—the very basics— things that didn't require a lot of assembly or reading rules. Without even realizing it, you settled for only *part* of the enjoyment your toy had to offer.

Getting the most out of your gift requires time, effort, and perhaps even a little creativity. You could have an ordinary experience with it, or you could have an incredible experience with it!

It kind of works the same way with your mom. The choice is up to you. Do you want a ho-hum, nothing special, let's-just-tolerate-each-other relationship, or do you want an honest, fun, and enjoyable relationship with her? Again, it's your choice.

"I love it when my mom comes to my basketball games and gets off work to do it."

—Rebekah, 17

This won't take a lot of time, but it *will* require some thoughtfulness. After all, it's the little things that will make what you and your mom share together memorable. So enjoy doing things such as:

- Saying hi to her when you walk in the door from school or when she comes home from work. Let her know you're genuinely happy to see her. And determine to smile when you talk with her!
- Surprise her once in a while by starting dinner or setting the

table before she gets home. That tells her you know she had a long day too.

- Leave a note on her bathroom counter wishing her a good day.
- Call her at work during lunch just to see how her day's going—not because you need something from her.
- Ask her how you can pray specifically for her today, and then do it!
- Do the dishes without being asked.
- Tell her about your day before she asks you about it.
- Thank her for cooking dinner or for doing your laundry.

Little expressions of "I noticed" and "I appreciate you" will mean more to your mom than you know. They'll also open the door to conversation between the two of you.

When your mom asks about your day, she's not being nosy; she just wants to talk to you. Enjoy the opportunity! She just wants to be included in what happens in your life at school, on the volleyball team, or at youth group. She's asking you to include her in your life when you're away from home. Be grateful that she wants to know about the fun things you're doing, whom you hang with, and what upsets you.

When *you* show interest in what happened during *her* day, it tells your mom that you see her as more than simply a parent who sets the rules and makes sure there's food in the refrigerator. It tells her that you see her as a

"My mom called me the day her father died. I was watching a movie and was distracted. I didn't ask her if she was okay, and we fought about it later. I apologized, and we talked about my trouble with showing empathy."

—Mari, 17

person with a life outside of yours, that you realize she has struggles and demands on her as well.

It also shows her that you recognize life isn't all about you. That's a major step of maturity on your part, and it reveals a beautiful truth: You're not a child anymore. You want a relationship with your mom beyond asking, "What's for dinner?" You want to learn from her life experience and be an encouragement to her when she needs it.

And after all, that's the goal—to move from a child-parent relationship to a friend-friend relationship. It doesn't happen overnight; it evolves over a period of time.

But half the fun is found in the process of getting there! So enjoy the process, and enjoy your mom while you have her.

Stuff I Could Never Tell My Daughter

- *I wasn't a virgin when I got married.*
- *Her father and I struggle in our marriage.*
- *I'm not as strong spiritually as I pretend to be.*
- *I was wrong.*
- *I attempted suicide when I was a teen.*
- *She scares me.*
- *I had an abortion.*
- *I don't feel loved.*
- *Many things frighten me.*
- *It's hard for me to pray.*
- *I struggle with depression.*

CHAPTER 14

Bumps Along the Way

The mother's heart is the child's schoolroom.
—Henry Ward Beecher

You've learned what it means to make a mother-daughter covenant and the power it has to bring you and your daughter into a closer relationship. Are you ready to jump in and give it your all?

Before you start living it out, let's get real. There *will* be some bumps along the way. You're still two different people from two different generations. You may prefer calming blue; your daughter's crazy about red and orange together. You enjoy classical music; she's into hip-hop. You may wish she were girlier, but she prefers ragged jeans and tennis shoes.

As you begin your journey of a covenant relationship with each other, it's very important that your expectations are prayerful and realistic. You both want a closer relationship, and you've agreed to do some things to help make that happen. But she's still a hormonal young girl living in a world of peer pressure, expectations, and the influence of a rapidly changing culture. You're still an adult looking back on your own teen years from a different perspective: Hindsight is 20/20.

Be patient. She'll still need your mother-mixture of toughness and tenderness. Will everything suddenly be smooth sailing for the two of you since you've made the covenant commitment?

Probably not.

Will you shed a few tears along the way?

Most likely.

Will you be disappointed and want to give up?

Maybe.

But hang in there! The end result is worth every ounce of energy you pour into it. Remember: Relationships take work. There may be times when you feel like you're the only one putting effort into this. Again, you're the adult—she's in the middle of tumultuous teen years.

The covenant commitment you're making is a sacred agreement between you, your daughter, and God. It'll take intentional effort, creativity, and flexibility to make it fulfilling.

It's a covenant for *life*, not just for a couple of weeks or until she moves out of the house or gets married.

It may take ferocious tenacity to maintain.

The task will seem overwhelming at times, but it will also be incredibly rewarding. God gave mothers the innate ability to have superhuman strength and determination when it comes to fighting for their children. Maybe you've heard the expression *"You don't mess with Mama's chickens!"* Our point exactly.

"I love it when my mom brushes my hair."

—Anna, 16

Actions Speak Louder Than Words

We've all heard the phrase *"What you are speaks so loudly I can't hear what you say."* That goes double for parents. Your daughter absorbs your mood swings, attitudes, unspoken vibes, and body language much faster than she does the words coming out of your mouth.

She knows who you really are behind closed doors. She was

there when the pasta boiled over and messed up your nice clean stove and when the garbage disposal backed up right before dinner guests were to arrive.

She watched your reaction when your husband forgot your birthday and when you got that speeding ticket. How you handle stress, disappointment, and heartache impacts how your daughter will learn to respond to life's difficulties. When problems come, don't expect her reaction to be more mature than your own. "Do as I say, not as I do" just doesn't cut it with teens.

Case in Point

Sheila expects her kids to obey their family rules, yet she argues with the principal about the three-tardies-and-you're-counted-absent rule at school. She shakes her fist at other drivers but jumps all over her kids when they're impatient with the person ahead of them in line at the checkout stand.

"I love it when my mom jokes with me."

—Amy, 13

If you don't model appropriate behavior to your daughter yet expect it of her, she may end up angry and resentful of your hypocrisy.

What can you do to make the most of the mother-daughter covenant experience?

Be Prepared

Know that you may end up carrying more than your equal share of the covenant commitment now and then. Your daughter's world is full of friends, friends' problems, and distractions. As the adult in this relationship, you may have to be the initiator to keep this covenant relationship growing. There may still be ups and downs in your relationship.

Be Committed

She may frustrate, exasperate, or disappoint you. Make sure she knows you're there for her. She'll need a place to go when life gets rough.

Determine to be a safe place for her to come to even if it means she wants to talk at 1:00 a.m. Be available to listen, wipe her tears, or share her excitement.

She may disappoint or hurt you in some way—but be forgiving and approachable. Wouldn't you rather have her come to you with her struggles than go to a boyfriend or classmate who doesn't care about her best interest half as much as you do?

Be Reminded

No matter how many rolled eyes or slammed doors you encounter along the way, these roller-coaster years are temporary. She won't be a teen forever.

Be Her Prayer Warrior

Pray for her daily. *Tell* her you pray for her. She faces outside influences every day that are shaping her life and who she'll become. Find out when that big test is. If it's second period, make sure she knows you'll be praying for her at that exact time. If she's having a problem with a teacher or friendship, be praying for her as she deals with it. Rejoice and praise God with her when those prayers are answered.

The idea of a covenant relationship may be terrifying to you.

Your stomach may be in knots at the thought of trying to connect with your daughter on a deeper level. If so, lay it at the feet of Jesus. God wants the two of you to share an amazing relationship. He will move heaven and earth to answer the fervent prayers of a mother's heart for her children.

She may not show it on the outside, but it gives your daughter great comfort to know you're praying for her. Pray in faith, believing God will work in her life. It may take time to see results, but God is faithful and has His watchful eye on your little girl.

What You Can Expect: Ages 11–14

There will be many changes in your daughter during these pre-teen and young teen years. Her body is changing, hormones are wacky, and she cries over the smallest things.

Twelve-year-old Kendra burst into tears because her brother said her new haircut made her look like the school librarian. Two weeks ago that would have had them both on the floor laughing hysterically. Today it's a major catastrophe.

"When my dad left, my mom and I grieved in different ways. She got clingy; I got cranky. We finally both talked about each other's emotions and moods and worked it out."

—Tabitha, 18

What used to be fun is now stupid. She communicates more with her body language and facial expressions than with words. You've suddenly become the most annoying person on the face of the earth and have no idea what you're talking about most of the time; at least that's how she perceives you today. Tomorrow may be totally different.

It's important to keep a few things in mind if you're going to navigate this awkward stage of your daughter's development without losing your mind and your temper.

She lives in a world that tells her to be way more grown-up and sophisticated than she's ready for. She wants to be older than she is and will try to dress and look older.

• Her friends are her lifelines to social acceptance. She'll want to spend more time with them than with you. This is totally normal.

She spends hours on the phone with them right after she gets home from seeing them at school all day.

- She really does want you involved in her life but doesn't want you to tell her what to do. She's developing her independence and wants to make more of her own decisions.

- She spends hours alone in her room behind closed doors. She's probably playing with new hairstyles and IMing her friends. She's trying to figure out who she's becoming. Her own life is morphing right before her eyes.

- She needs clear boundaries. Her friends and the culture are telling her she should be mature and cutting her ties with you, but she's not yet capable of making logical decisions on her own. Her choices are more influenced by outside sources than ever before. She needs you to protect her from her own immaturity and inexperience.

    Give her a little more freedom as she can handle it—in gradual stages. Keep close watch on who and what is influencing her choices.

- She may be boy crazy. She sees some of her friends dating and having boy-girl parties, and it looks like fun. She wants attention from boys and may dress or act inappropriately to get it.

Andrea looked up from the ironing board one day to see her clean-faced ponytailed adolescent daughter run up to her room after school only to return to the dinner table with chopped-off hair, raccoon eyes, and her shirt cut off halfway up her belly. What happened? A new girl moved to her school who had all the boys turning their heads and fighting over

"I love it when my mom respects my privacy."

—Kendall, 16

who would sit by her at lunch. She looked like a rock star at eleven years old.

Fireworks flew when Andrea made her daughter go right back upstairs and wash her face and put on some decent clothes. The rest of the family laughed. Slammed doors and tears followed accusations of "You never understand!"

Those kinds of outbursts have come with regularity for the past few months. Andrea wonders if life will ever be normal at their house again. She has two younger daughters coming right along behind this stormy one.

Sigh.

Encourage your adolescent daughter that it's okay to have boys who are friends and not to be in a hurry for a boyfriend. Don't push her to dress older than she is or wear more makeup than is appropriate for her age. She's attracting male attention that she is not ready for. Caution her about Internet predators and friendly older teen guys and men who may want to give her the wrong kind of attention.

• She may be sassy. The friends she chooses to hang out with are a huge influence on how she acts, talks, and respects or disrespects you and others in authority. Know who her friends are. Don't be afraid to intervene if you see inappropriate choices in friends at this impressionable age. They are shaping who she's becoming— big time.

• She's insecure in her body image. Help her celebrate her femininity and changing body. She may be developing before her friends or she may be a late bloomer. Both are embarrassing.

Help her through this awkward stage. If her skin is breaking out, take her to a dermatologist or ask your pharmacist for over-the-counter treatments. If her crooked teeth are an embarrassment to her, bite the bullet and invest in braces.

Whatever you can do to help her feel comfortable in her own

skin at this age is well worth the cost. This is a critical age for building self-confidence.

- Celebrate rights of passage. Teenagers don't need much of a reason for a party. Make every accomplishment or milestone in her life a reason to celebrate. Give her goals to look forward to and work toward: starting to wear makeup, making the honor roll or getting a part in the school play, committing to a purity pledge, and eventually taking driver's ed. All are cause for celebration. Life should be fun as you enter the teen years together!

What You Can Expect: Ages 15–16

This is a fun stage of your daughter's life. She's become more confident, and her talents and areas of interest are narrowing down. You're seeing her make more mature decisions and take on more responsibility.

She's probably very involved in extracurricular activities at school or church and keeps you busy carpooling,

"I love it when my mom has midnight snacks with me and chats."

—Evelyn, 17

at least until she gets that coveted driver's license! The very thought both scares you to death and excites you as she can now get herself places without your needing to be the chauffeur.

Her friends are an integral part of her life, and she spends more time out of the house than in. She's become more comfortable in her young woman's body and the hormones have settled a bit.

Your role as Mom is changing too. Now's the time to step back a little and watch your blossoming daughter become who she was uniquely created to be.

You can count on bumps to come if you continue to treat her as if she were eleven or twelve years old. In case you hadn't noticed, she's not a child anymore. Parenting needs to change when your daughter becomes a teenager. Threats of punishment for not making her bed or leaving a mess in the kitchen will go in one ear and out the other. She wants to be respected and talked to like an adult, not a child.

She still needs you—perhaps more than ever. She may experience her first date at this age and ask you to help her shop for her first prom dress.

Things may have smoothed out from the tumultuous middle-school years, or you may be in the heat of battle as the two of you get used to her being more independent and away from home so much.

Here are a few tips to help you stay connected with her:

"*My mom has been grieving for two years because my older sister turned from God. It's like my mom just died and hasn't really been there for me. I think we're healing now, but the wound is so deep. I had to truly open myself up to her, which was very hard!*"

—Tressa, 16

• Step into her world and find out what she loves. She may have totally different interests than you; try to encourage her to develop her strengths and hobbies even if they're totally foreign to you.

Don't try to make her into a carbon copy of yourself or another sibling. If she loves hiking, hike with her. If she enjoys writing, read her work and encourage her to develop her talent. If she's into gymnastics or drama, be her biggest cheerleader. If she likes to tinker with motors, let her! She's one of a kind. Give her permission to be who she is wired by God to be.

- Get to know her. Tap into her personality and discover what motivates her. There is no one-size-fits-all parenting. You may have three daughters and each one of them is completely different. Don't expect them to be motivated by the same things. Spend time with each one individually and study her personalities, abilities, and areas of interest. Encourage each one where she is gifted. Tell her how much you enjoy spending time with her.
- Encourage her to seek God's plan for her life. This is the time she'll start thinking about her future. It's a scary thing to try to figure out who she is and what she's made for with so many options out there to choose from. Guide her in discovering her talents and encourage her in those things.
- Make your home a fun place to be. Always have your door open to her friends for after-the-game hangouts and pizza parties. Teens need safe places to congregate on weekends and for after-school activities.

  Don't worry that your house isn't clean or big enough—they just want to be together. You can provide a warm and friendly environment right in your home for them to watch movies, play games, and raid your refrigerator. It doesn't take much—give them your basement and something to eat and you'll have the most popular house in town!
- Bless her with faith in her success. Whether she makes the basketball team or gets a C on the test she was sure she failed, give your daughter the blessing of your faith in her. Maybe she had to take her driver's test twice before passing—make a big deal of her success rather than remind her that she failed it the first time.

Help Yourself Out

There are some things you can do to make this letting-go transition easier on yourself as the mom of a teen girl. Take advantage of the experience of one who's been there. Here are a few things I (Kathy) have learned after raising both a teen son and a teen daughter.

First, don't expect mature behavior from an immature teen. The frontal lobe of the human brain where impulse control is housed is not fully developed until age twenty-five. Your daughter will not be capable of always making wise and logical decisions until then. Many adults still don't have the discipline to keep from making impulsive decisions. Keep in mind your daughter is still a teenager, not yet an adult. Make sure your expectations are age-appropriate no matter how mature you think your daughter is.

> "I love it when my mom tells me what she struggled with when she was my age."
>
> —Michelle, 16

Hopefully long before she's fifteen you've talked about what you and your husband feel is an appropriate age for her to start dating. Whenever that first date happens, it opens up a whole new set of things for you to worry about—the very fact that she's out with a teen driver, let alone the physical temptations that come with being hormonal teens, curfews, and not knowing where she is at all times. The dating years can be very stressful.

Take it from a mom who's been there twice: You'll do yourself a big favor if you focus on the positives of your teen's dating years rather than drive yourself crazy with worry about all the "what ifs."

Have some guidelines set in advance—it will save both you and your daughter a lot of grief. Establish a clear curfew that is reasonable before she goes on that first date. When will you expect her home? It will help her know what you expect and will help you relax if she's not home by ten-thirty when you've given her a curfew of eleven.

When our kids were teens, we made it standard practice that they would come into our bedroom and wake us up to tell us when they came home from a date or a night out with friends. That kept them accountable to their curfew time and gave Mom and Dad a couple hours of restful sleep before they came in, knowing we didn't have to wait up for them to be sure they got home safely.

As we talked about in chapter 10, it's important to have a plan for communication. Make sure your daughter has a cell phone or some way to contact you in case of an emergency or just to tell you the movie got out late and she won't be home exactly on time. A simple phone call can put your mind at ease and diffuse a lot of conflict. You may even go so far as to have a code word that she can use at any time that simply means *"Come get me, NOW"!* No questions asked—you can talk about it later. It means she needs to be rescued from an uncomfortable situation.

What You Can Expect: Ages 17–19

At this age, Mom needs to step back even more. Your daughter's out or nearly out of high school and on to college or a full-time job. She's now considered an adult by society and is taking more responsibility for herself and the consequences of her choices.

"I love it when my mom takes me to cool thrift stores."

—Becki, 17

She needs your guidance now more than your lectures. If she gets a speeding ticket, she pays the fine. If she decides to go to college a thousand miles away from home, she'll live with the fact that she can't come home every other weekend.

She'll need your help thinking through decisions that she'll ultimately be responsible for. Your life experience will be a valuable asset as you talk through these things.

She wants you to talk *to* her, not *at* her. She wants your input but needs to make her own decisions. You're moving closer to friendship with her, and it will delight you more than you know to stand back and look at the beautiful sight in front of you: your maturing young adult daughter. You've nearly made it through the teen years!

Still, there are things that will come up between you. Here are a few to be prepared for:

Healthy Versus Unhealthy Relationships

The very essence of womanhood thrives on loving and being loved. How she learns to do this has been largely influenced by what she has learned from you and watching your relationship with her father. If that has been an unhealthy relationship or her father has passed away or isn't in the home, she may be looking for male attention in unhealthy ways.

If this has become apparent in your daughter's life, your most effective weapon against this scenario will be prayer. She's looking for validation from a man, someone to tell her she's beautiful, feminine, and desirable.

If her dad isn't in the home to impart a healthy self-esteem in her as a woman, encourage her to set her sights high in this important area of her personal life. You can do this by giving her some simple guidelines in what to look for in a boyfriend or future husband. Come up with your own list, but here are a few to get you started:

- Does he respect you as a person, or see you as a "trophy"?
- Is he interested in your thoughts, ideas, and preferences about where you go to eat or what you do on your dates, or is he only interested in what he wants to do?
- Does he notice when you're sad, worried, or upset about something? Does he try to comfort you?
- How does he introduce you to his friends? Does he even bother?
- How does he treat his mother? He'll most likely treat you the same way. The beloved humor writer Erma Bombeck once said, "Spend at least one Mother's Day with your respective mothers

before you decide on marriage. If a man gives his mother a gift certificate for a flu shot, dump him." Erma was a wise woman!

- Does he bring out the best in you and encourage you to be all you can be?
- Does he treat you like a lady—opening doors for you, pulling out your chair before you sit down—or do you follow him, trying not to get hit by the door on your way in?

Assure her of her precious worth and value as a woman uniquely created by God. She should be careful about whom she gives her heart to and willing to wait for God's best in her dating life.

"I love it when my mom knows when I've had a bad day."

—Randi, 14

Wings to Fly

Know when it's time for her to use her wings and fly. There have been two major milestones for my mother-heart besides giving our son away in marriage and having our first grandchild. They were the first day of kindergarten and driving away after moving the kids into a college dorm. Both were major letting-go moments for me. I had released them from my care to manage on their own in new environments—one just down the street and the other a thousand miles away from home. Both were equally traumatizing!

In the first scenario, I had taught them how to tie their shoes, say please and thank-you, and not to talk to strangers. In the second, it was how to manage their money, use an automated bank card, and book an airline ticket. My baby was now an adult going out into an adult world to do adult things. It was both exhilarating and frightening!

It's much easier to let your daughter go when you know you've done all you can do to prepare her for the day she'll walk out of your house to a life on her own. There's peace in knowing you've done your job and prepared her well.

Think About It

- Looking back on the bumps in the road with your daughter, what could you have done differently to make the ride smoother?
- It's never too late to repair damage done. Is there something you need to apologize to your daughter about to restore your connection?
- When's the last time you and your daughter did something together, just the two of you?
- Does your daughter know how proud you are of her?

Here for You Journal Entries

This is a fun way to keep the communication lines between the two of you open. Buy, make, or designate a specific notebook that you can pass between yourselves that will be known as your mom-daughter journal.

We've started with some simple, non-threatening, general statements that can be completed by either mom *or* daughter (or both!). You'll notice, however, as we get a little further along in the communication process, we've designated specific questions from the daughters for moms to answer and specific questions from the mom for her daughter to answer.

This is something you do at your own pace. Don't rush each other. Some may want to do it every day; others may take a week to answer one set of questions. That's okay. It's not the time limit that's important; it's the process of communication that's valued.

When you've completed the questions we've suggested, start making up your own. Feel free to get as creative as you want: cut something fun out of a magazine and glue it to the page; attach a favorite photo of the two of you on a page and ask the responder to write the memories and feelings associated with the photo. The sky's the limit!

- If I could color happiness, it would be _____
  _____.
- If I could have dinner with anyone in history, it would be
  _____, because _____.
- I love the smell of _____.

- If I could vacation anywhere in the world, I'd go to _____ _____.
- My favorite food is _____.
- When I'm sad, I want to be _____.

- Thinking of _____ makes me laugh.
- Thinking of _____ makes me cry.
- My favorite movie is _____.

- More than anything, I want my mom/daughter to know that I _____.
- I love it when she _____.
- One smell that brings back memories is _____ _____.

- My favorite room in our house is _____.
- I'm afraid of _____.
- These are my favorite sounds: (list them)

- I always laugh when you _____.
- One of my favorite childhood books was _____ _____.
- I love my _____.

- My favorite flower is _____.
- I get really stressed when _____.
- When I'm stressed I need _____.

- Two of my pet peeves: _____, _____.
- I love to _____ to relax.
- One thing I'd like to have done differently in my life is _____.

- I need to know I'm _____.
- _____ really embarrasses me.
- Stuff I think is fun:

- My best friend is _____.
- One of my favorite family memories is _____.
- I hate it when _____.
- My favorite teacher was _____ because

  _____.

- I'm proud of you because _____.
- One food I could eat every day of my entire life is _____.
- One food I would rather not see again in my entire life is

  _____.

- I would rather ride: a unicycle by myself / a tandem bike for two. (Circle one.)
- I chose that one because _____.
- If I could have three wishes, I would wish for:

- One thing I wish you understood better about me is _____

  _____.
- My favorite childhood toy was _____.
- This is a Scripture verse or poem I have memorized:

- I think being real means _____.
- I admire _____ because _____

  _____.
- I would love to learn how to _____.

- One place I want to visit before I die is _____.
- My favorite place to eat is _____.
- My dream car would be a _____.

- My favorite Christmas gift ever was _____.
- I need to tell _____ I'm sorry for _____
  _____.
- If I had to compare my family to a car, it would be a _____
  _____ because _____.

- If someone paid me to dye my hair pink and keep it that way for
  two weeks, I would do it for $_____.
- A recent answer to prayer was _____.
- One goal I want to accomplish in the next year is _____.

- If I had a horse, I'd name it _____.
- One thing I like about my body is _____.
- I love being _____.

- I think I have good _____.
- I wish I could change my _____.
- My favorite meal my mother cooks(ed) is _____.

- I love _____ cake.
- My favorite green vegetable is _____.
- If I could create a new flavor of chewing gum, it would be
  _____.

- If I could do one thing over it would be _____
  _____.
- The last time I cried was _____.
- I love _____ movies.

- I have _____ dreams.
- My favorite way to eat chicken is _____.
- If I were a millionaire, I would _____.
- I would *never* wear _____ with _____.

- On weekends I like to _____.
- When I'm upset I like to be _____.
- I absolutely hate the smell of _____.

- My favorite amusement park ride is _____.
- I _____ cotton candy.
- My favorite things that are red: (list them)

- My favorite place to shop is _____.
- Something I've learned about you since we started journaling is _____.
- I'm so proud of my _____ because _____.

- _____ bores me.
- _____ excites me!
- _____ is my favorite hobby.

- I'm better than average at _____.
- I wish I knew _____ better.
- I wish _____ would really listen to me.

- I love to make people feel _____.
- I don't think _____ really understands me.
- I pray for _____.

- My heart breaks over _____.
- I love to hear _____ laugh.
- I've never liked the taste of _____.

- True or False (circle one): I could have made it as a pioneer woman.
- I'm a natural _____.
- I would like to learn how to _____.

- I love it when _____ hugs me.
- These are eight of my favorite things: (list them)
- The first thing I do when I wake up in the morning is _____
  _____.

- The smell of _____ always reminds me of
  _____.
- If I could trade places with *anybody* in all of history for one day,
  it would be _____ because _____
  _____.
- My favorite TV show is _____.

- I'm a morning / night person. (Circle one.)
- I don't like to be bothered when I'm _____.
- _____ really irritates me.

- The accomplishment I am most proud of is _____
  _____.
- Daughters: I want to marry a man who _____
  _____.
- I was so embarrassed when _____.

- I hate / love pantyhose because _____.
- My favorite season is _____ because
  _____.
- Christmas shopping makes me _____.

- I love to _____.
- I know more about _____ than _____
  _____.
- I once got in trouble for _____.

- I've never told you before that _____.
- Here's why I love my hair, in exactly twenty-one words:
- I wish I had thought of _____.

- True or False (circle one): I read my Bible this week.
- I wish I had more time to _____.
- I made _____ feel good about himself/herself this week.

- I'm glad I _____.
- I'm sorry I _____.
- It feels good to know you ___ _____.

- I admire your ability to _____.
- I never laughed as hard as when _____.
- I would eat _____ if it tasted like _____.

- I want to be a _____ mother.
- Here's how I describe the color blue:
- The best book I ever read was _____.

- This week I've wanted to be _____.
- I'd rather eat a _____ than sleep on a _____.
- Six words to describe me that start with the letter L: (list them)

- Wearing _____ makes me feel beautiful.
- My favorite perfume is _____.
- If I could live in another country, I'd move to _____ _____.

- I believe I can _____.
- I'm really good at _____.
- I stink at _____.

Daughter Asks, Mom Answers

- What people skills do you see in me?

- What do you think my friends appreciate most about me?

- What will make me a great mom someday?

Mom Asks, Daughter Answers

- How can I help you know even more that I love you, believe in you, and support you?

- If you could ask me anything, what would it be?

- What's your favorite thing for the two of us to do together?

Daughter Asks, Mom Answers

- What kind of man do you hope I'll marry someday?

- What quality do you see in me that will make me a great wife?

- How will I know who God wants me to marry?

Mom Asks, Daughter Answers

- If you could build a house for our family, what would it be like? Describe it.

- If you could be the best at anything in the world, what would you choose to excel in?

- If you were to write a book, what would you title it?

Daughter Asks, Mom Answers

- What's one thing you regret about your teen years?

- What's something you loved about your teen years?

- If you were a teen right now and we weren't related, would you choose me as your friend? Why or why not?

Mom Asks, Daughter Answers

- What frustrates you most about our relationship?

- What do you value most about our relationship?

- What do you love most about our relationship?

Daughter Asks, Mom Answers

- What's your favorite thing for the two of us to do together?

- Why did you give me the name you gave me?

- If you could choose another name for yourself, what would it be?

Mom Asks, Daughter Answers

- If you could choose another name for yourself, what would it be?

- What are the top three qualities you want in your future husband?

- If you could ask God anything, what would you ask Him?

Daughter Asks, Mom Answers

- Where'd you go and what did you do on your first date?

- When I was born, what was going on in the world at that time?

- If there's one thing you want to make sure I learn, what is it?

Mom Asks, Daughter Answers

- What's the most difficult thing for you to talk with me about?
- Would you rather have to hop on one foot for every tenth word you speak or rhyme every tenth word you speak?

- If there's one thing you want to make sure I know, what is it?

To order your own

Here for You necklaces,

custom designed for this

mother-daughter covenant experience,

go to:

www.closermomsanddaughters.com.